Published by: Tracey Jefferson

Editing and Graphic Design: Karen Bowlding

Cover Photos Credit: avemario

ISBN: 978-0-692-18705-0

Library of Congress: 2018960272

DEDICATION

This book is dedicated to my son, Stephen. Thank you for trusting me as I trusted Christ to walk out alive.

-

It's also dedicated to the women and men that have suffered in silence and to those that are still suffering in silence due to domestic violence. I hope my truth can aid in helping you to decide to know your worth and value. I'm rooting for you to survive!

It's also dedicated to the abusers. This is a learned behavior. I'm sorry that you are suffering in your own way due to someone who may have abused you as a kid or young adult. Please confide in someone and get help!

ACKNOWLEGEMENTS

I would like to express my sincere gratitude to my friends, mainly my BFF Joyce Watson, for being upset with me when I went back. I know it was not easy for you to accept, however, I needed to make sure I did everything I could as a godly wife before leaving for good. Thank you for being concerned about me and I love you for that.

To my co-workers who allowed me to confide in them while I was suffering: Some of you didn't know what I was going through, however, your words and acts of kindness and all the laughs we shared, helped me enjoy some peace of mind, even if it was at work. It really meant a lot to me. Thank you!

To the hardest working woman in Washington, D.C. Metropolitan (DMV) area, Carolyn White-Washington: I reached out to her for assistance about my book and Carolyn didn't hesitate to give me the name of the best editor in the DMV, Karen Bowlding. Thank you ladies for being patient, kind, and with a heart to serve.

-

To my church family during that time, Free Gospel Deliverance Temple, Bishop Ralph E and son Wayne Green: I made it through because of the preached word. Thank you for the free counseling sessions from the pulpit. I miss you so very much Bishop!

-

I also would like to thank my family, mainly my niece Ronetta (Ronnie). I'm sorry that I didn't confide in you, mainly because I knew you would've taken matters into your own hands and probably, would be just coming out of jail. Please know, I had to grow up and allow God be God in that situation, so please forgive me. I love very much.

-

To the Charles County Police Department: thank you so much for your protection and kindness towards me and my son. You all made me feel safe.

-

My mother truly suffered in her own silence while still managing to raise seven children. I believe that I am great because of her. I always wanted her to be proud of me. I believe that she was, and she showed it by her deep and unconditional love for the both of us.

-

Although my dad wasn't in my life, I still unconditionally love him.

-

Lastly, the love of my life, you all know who that is, Yes, my son, Stephen. I am getting choked up just trying to put into words how grateful I am for you. Thank you for your forgiveness towards me, thank you for your patience with me, and thank you for trusting and believing in me. Thank you for the man that you have become!

I love you all so very much,

Tracey J.

INTRODUCTION

It was 5:30 on December 30, 1996, the morning of our first wedding anniversary. I was propped in my favorite resting position in our bedroom, watching television with my husband lying next to me.

I greeted him with a pleasant, "Good morning."

He greeted me with his teeth clinched ever so tightly and evil in his eyes, asking, "Who is he? Who are you sleeping with?"

Before I could respond, he was on top of me with his hands around my throat, choking the life out of me.

He said again, "You better tell me. Who you are sleeping with?"

As the breath began to leave my limp body, I reached up to touch his face. I can remember smiling and thinking calmly, "Well Lord, is this how my life ends?" My next thought was that of my ten-year-old son. Who would tell him the truth? At that point, the nightmare began. Welcome to *Suffering in Silence.*

TABLE OF CONTENTS

-CHAPTER ONE-
WHO I WAS

I was born April 30, 1962, the youngest of seven children to my mother, the late Doris Jefferson, and my father, the late Charles James Jefferson. I prefer to be known as the baby of the family. I grew up in what some people might call the worst part of Washington, D.C., southeast to be exact. We lived in a small house where we mainly used our back door more than the front. Those projects were better known as Barry Farms Dwellings. I loved living there. When we moved from Stevens Road, I was only six years old, but I had the most memorable of memories in that house. I went past that house and prayed for the people living there. I wondered if they like living there as much as I did. My sister, friends, and I had a lot of fun. We used to have alley dances. All the neighbors gathered together, and the music was being pumped in the alley. We met all of our friends and sat on our back porch because my mother didn't allow us to go into the alley. My older sisters and brothers met friends, and they hand danced along with making out once it got dark.

We had so much fun while living in Barry Farms. Many times, my sister, two other girls, and I waited for all the other people to go into their houses. We then went up to the well-lit spot on the field where we did the sweater dance. We pulled our sweaters on our heads and pretended that we were a famous singing group. The sweaters were used to imitate long hair. We turned and swayed our hair and sang our hearts out. That was so much fun! Usually, about fifteen minutes into the singing, Momma called for us to come in the house.

"Pammy and Tracey, get your butts in this house. You know the street lights are on."

"Aw man, here she come again. Dang, she always makes us all come in all early."

We huffed and puffed under our breath and got our butts in that house. We were still excited because we knew we would do it again the next day.

I thought that life in the Farms was good. It really wasn't that good. I didn't know any better. My family had its secrets. As the youngest, I didn't know that my older sisters and brother were getting into trouble. Normally, we found out those things after a certain age. My sisters and brothers' names, starting with the oldest to me, are: Janis, Jeannette (a.k.a. Jean), Charles, Gary, Patricia (a.k.a. Patsy or Pat), Pamela (a.k.a. Pammy). Now that Pammy is all grown, we call her Pam. And, finally, there is me, Tracey.

I didn't get to know my father while growing up, but one thing I do remember about him is that he was very handsome, dressed nicely, wore nice cologne, and he smoked cigars. Even to this day, I love to smell them. I often think that since I didn't have my father around, it may have been why I struggled to find a good man or why I had problems in my life. I really wish that I had a relationship with him or gotten to know him. I didn't even know his favorite color. The things I knew about my dad was that he loved baseball and women. He cheated on my mother several times and fathered a ton of children, a total of fourteen, and there may be more. I always felt some kind of way when I learned about men who fathered children and didn't take care of them. I wondered why, but I later realized that it was because my dad was not there for me. If he was sober when I called, we talked about school and what day he was coming to see me. Do I hate men who neglect their families? Am I bitter because of this? I don't believe so. It's amazing to me how some people can be attracted to someone who constantly abuses them, mentally and physically, and they still want that person to be a part of their life. My father abused my mother. Did I follow in her footsteps? Did I marry a man just like my father?

-

Have you ever made a list of the type of man you want to spend the rest of your life with—the man you want to marry? I had a list. I wrote my expectations. The man of my dreams had to:

- have one or two children and didn't want anymore
- have a job
- be very handsome
- know how to cook
- enjoy being with my son
- be tall
- have all of his teeth
- have a car
- be funny, able to make me laugh

After looking over my list, I was amused. What type of criteria were those? Don't laugh. I bet your criteria is worse than mine. What are your criteria? Please answer honestly. If you are with someone, be it your spouse, fiancé, or someone you are just dating, does he/she meet your standards? If so, praise God for him/her and tell them how fortunate you are to have him/her in your life. If he/she doesn't, then keep reading, because this book is for you!

I believe that I'm a fairly beautiful woman. I love to laugh. I can handle joking around and sometimes being the life of the party. When I was about twenty-one years old, I wore a size four. However, my personality was awful. I had to have things done my way. When not done according to my rules, I did it myself, and considered the person to be inadequate—useless. I didn't allow room for errors. I also hated to repeat myself. When I had to say something more than twice, I boiled over with anger. Whoever was on the receiving end of my tirade got it good. I then disappeared from their life. I was very selfish and arrogant.

I shopped all the time, whenever possible. I purchased matching shoes and handbags with every outfit. Everything had to be lined up and coordinated, if not, I didn't feel comfortable. Outwardly, I truly had it all together—full of vainglory. I was insecure. I scolded people, sometimes for minor reasons. When I was wrong, instead of apologizing, I became defensive and blamed them, which often led to arguments. I don't recall ever asking for forgiveness or forgiving others. I meant what I said and said what I meant. Even when I knew the person was right, I didn't back down. After I had done or said something that may have hurt someone's feelings, I didn't care. I habitually lied for no apparent reason, other than to get my own way. Or, did I really get my way?

I dated brothers, stepbrothers, roommates, neighbors, and coworkers. When I called someone, and one wasn't home, I conversed with the other and the rest is history. I reasoned in my mind that I wasn't hurting anyone. I can now admit that I was empty inside.

Continuing to confess, I dated married men. Some I knew were married, others I didn't, and several claimed to be separated. Yes, I fell for lies. Frequently, I went to nightclubs knowing I didn't have a ride, I expected to meet someone who would take me home. During that time, it was the 1980s and the crime wasn't bad. It was fun. My girlfriend and I competed to see how many men and phone numbers we could get by the end of the night. Believe it or not, I always had the most. She might disagree with me, but this is my book and my story, so go along with me. I'm glad that we are still friends.

The club scene was beginning to get a little boring. I was in my early twenties and wanted to settle down. I rented my own apartment and was ready to come home to someone. The men I dated during that time weren't marriage material and neither was I. However, I managed to narrow them all down to one. He was the love of my life. He showered me with pearls, watches, and fun. He was honest enough to tell me he was married and only had several months to go before his divorce was final. Just before the month was over, he went back to his wife, leaving me crushed and alone. Because I was hurting, I decided to relocate to San Francisco, California in 1984. I had relatives who lived there that I rarely got to see. My cousin, Prestola Mayberry, was up in age and I wanted to help her. She looked forward to my arrival.

I purchased plane ticket and gave the rental office and my job a thirty-day notice. I had one more thing to do before I was to leave the Washington, D.C. area. I visited my obstetrician and gynecologist to have a final check-up and get a supply of birth control pills to last until I could locate a new doctor. My visit to the doctor was normal. I continued to carry on with my plans to move. I received a call from my doctor, and he informed me that I was pregnant. Although we had a good relationship, I told him that the report was wrong, and he had the wrong patient. We both laughed. He was adamant and advised me to come in for a blood test. Remember, I was never wrong. I did as he requested. He was correct. I was seven weeks pregnant. I wondered how it could have happened. I faithfully took my birth control pills. That was truly the last thing in the world I wanted or needed. I was twenty-two years old. "I'm too selfish to have a baby," I thought.

Because I didn't want to have a baby, I called my doctor to schedule a "you-know-what". He stated that he didn't perform that type of procedure, but recommended someone who did. I cried the whole weekend. In my innermost being, I didn't want to have an abortion. I called a dear friend to tell her. I didn't understand why or how she could be happy for me.

On Monday morning, she picked me up for work. In the front seat of her red car were the Sunday inserts with an inventory of baby products that were on sale.

With a wide smile on her face, she said, "We are going to look at some cribs this afternoon."

I looked at her and responded, "I am not going to have this baby. I'm having an abortion."

The look on her face was one of disgust. She told me off…and I mean bad. Back then, I had not been told off by a woman before who had gotten away with it. Under no uncertain terms was she going to allow me to have an abortion.

I rescinded my notice, unpacked my apartment, canceled my plane ticket, and informed my cousin that I wasn't coming. She was disappointed and cussed at me, however, my mother was delighted. She was going to be a grandmother for the tenth time. My sister Jean was also happy. I believed that because I was having a child, I could better prioritize my life. I began to settle down and made wiser decisions.

CHAPTER TWO

CRUSHED EXPECTATIONS

At the age of twenty-four, I purchased my first home. My son was two years old at the time. I didn't grow up in an apartment, and I felt that my son shouldn't either. I purchased a home that was one home away from my sister Jean's house. She was happy that I was moving so close. Every evening, my son waited at my bedroom window for her to come home from work. Most evenings, she took him with her to go shopping at the local department stores. My sister Jean and my mother competed to see who could buy my son the most things.

During that time, my best friend Joyce, my sister Jean, and I went to discos. We followed who was the hottest disc jockey during that time. Wherever he was, we were there. Because he played a lot of our favorite songs, we stayed on the dance floor for hours. I was so vain. I practiced dance moves in the mirror to see what I looked like while dancing. It was important to always be cool and smooth. I also did that to learn which moves

I could make to keep my hair from frizzing into a giant bush by the end of the night. That hairstyle wasn't fashionable in the 80s.

After a while of hanging out at the club, I was beginning to get bored again. I didn't understand what was happening. I felt empty. I had a good job, nice home, plenty of men, and looked good. I was just going through the motions. I wondered, "If the club scene wasn't satisfying, then it could've been the job I'd had for the past ten years." In search of a new and exciting career, I explored job openings in the newspaper. I made a few calls and landed an interview the next day. I got the job. I resigned and started what I hoped to be a new and exciting career with a brokerage firm as an insurance broker.

A change at last. Is this what I needed? Within two weeks, my excitement turned into dismay. I should've known that something was wrong when I only performed receptionist duties. Not to demean the job title, but I was not hired to answer the phone and take messages. During the interview, he informed me that I would be writing and or selling insurance policies to small business owners.

When I questioned him about going out to the companies, he always said, "Soon."

While speaking with a coworker, she informed me the owner of the company told another business owner that I was his niece.

He stated to someone else that I was his girlfriend. The real clincher was when the state insurance commissioner called and informed me that my boss was operating an illegal insurance business. I took my personal folder out of his file cabinet and quickly left. I didn't look back. While driving home, all I could think about was that it was another unfulfilled venture. I questioned where I would go and what I would do. Not only was I still empty, I was also unemployed.

I started going to church for the first time in my adult life. On April 9, 1989 while at the Free Gospel Deliverance Temple Church, I met the One who completely changed my life. He was Jesus Christ. One Sunday after service, I went to visit my mom. She sat on the side of her full-sized bed wearing a flowered housedress. The fragrance of perfume lingered in the air. We felt the gentle breeze coming through her window. She was happy to see me and proud that I was attending church. When I told her about the sermon, I suddenly began to bitterly weep. The guilt and shame I felt because of the way I was living had finally caught up with me. My mother would've been disappointed in me if she had known about the nasty things I had done. Yuck, I still get a sick feeling when I think about it. I thank Jesus for his grace and mercy!

My mom gave me my first Bible. It was a green covered book entitled *The Book*. I still have it. Although the pages have fallen apart, I cherish it because my mother's original handwritten notes are in it.

It was remarkable when I gave my life to the Lord. I was transformed. People couldn't believe that I was the same person. I purposely controlled myself instead of reacting out of emotions and cussing someone out. When confrontation arose, I was the first to apologize. Some nonbelievers waited for me to slip up and say something that the old Tracey would've said. I didn't give them the opportunity to criticize me. It was amazing to me how people didn't believe a person could change for the better. Well, I did and I am living proof that God is a deliverer.

In the beginning, my walk with the Lord was scary. I could no longer have sexual intercourse. Oh, my goodness! "This is going to be torture," I thought. I could no longer go to the clubs and there was to be no more dancing in the mirror, practicing my dance moves.

I cried out one day and asked the Lord what I could do besides read my Bible and listen to gospel music. After a while, that also became boring. Because I had come from a life of lust, alcohol, and shame, my flesh screamed and craved for some, if not all, of those sins. I gave up. I pulled out my telephone book. I wanted to call up some male friends—just to talk, nothing else. I tried to convince myself that I *only* wanted to talk.

One day, as I sat in my Oriental-styled living room, I prayed and asked God to help me. I was feeling low and no longer wanting to fornicate. I prayed and cried out to God. Once I stopped crying, The Lord gave me a parable. It was a vision of a fire place mantle. On top of the mantle was a pack of cigarettes. When someone wanted to stop smoking, what is the first thing they need to do? They need to get rid of the cigarettes. The cigarettes equated to the men in my telephone book. I leaped up from my couch. It was a clear indication to me that I should get rid of my little black book. I trashed the book and drove to the nearest convenience store to purchase a new phone book. Once I recorded the numbers of my family and very close friends, those whom I wanted to call, I realized the book was quite empty. I could have written those numbers on a sheet of notebook paper. Well, at least I got rid of the temptation.

Late one midnight hour, I tossed in my bed. The idea of making a booty call came to mind. I still remembered a close friend's phone number. He was a city worker and his number was embedded in my memory. I could dial his number in the dark. Well, the Lord had another idea. When my flesh got weak, I reached for the telephone to call him. At that moment, my mind went completely blank.

Then I heard the Lord say, "I will keep you if you want to be kept."

That was an experience I will not forget.

I cried and told the Lord, "Yes, please keep me."

Even though I cried myself to sleep, the sleep was sweet. God was so gentle. I woke up happy. Fornication was just one of my many sins. I began to prosper and was feeling free! No more bondage!

I called my previous manager to let her know that the job didn't work out.

She said, "So, when do you want to come back?

I said, "Today."

We both laughed, and she said, "Let's start on Monday."

In May of 1989, I went back to my old job. God was so good!

Since I was a believer in Christ, it meant no more drinking. I gave my sister Jean all of the beer and wine I had stored. She was amazed that I stopped. While talking in my kitchen, I invited her to come to church with me and my son. She came and truly enjoyed herself. Once service was over, we stood under the hot sun and talked about her experience. She said she wanted to go down to the front when the pastor had the altar call, but got scared. I told her that it was normal. We talked more, then hugged, and both drove home.

One beautiful morning, as I was leaving for work, an old classmate drove past my house and blew her horn. I waved and wondered how she was feeling since her only sister had passed away several weeks before. When the thought dropped into my head that I would soon find out, I questioned why I could think such an evil thought. Nothing was wrong with any of my sisters. I shared my thought with a Christian woman on my job. She tried to make sense of it. She took my hands and started praying for me and my family.

The next day, was June 30, 1989, two months after my new life in Christ. I received a call from one of my sisters while I was at work. She informed me that my sister Jean, my best friend, party buddy, neighbor, the sister my son waited in the window every day to see, had slipped into a coma. I immediately became lightheaded and screamed. It was devastating news. In a panic, I tried to leave work. A coworker decided to drive me to the hospital. I hadn't prayed and cried so hard in my life. We didn't know how to get to the hospital. We saw a policeman on his motorcycle, flagged him down, and informed him about where we were going. He noticed I was extremely emotional and had so much compassion toward me that he escorted us through the traffic.

I was still a babe in Christ, and I didn't quite know what to do. So, I called a friend and co-worker to inform her while at the hospital. She and her husband had been instrumental in my life. They decided to call the church. They were able to reach the bishop, and I informed him about what was happening. He prayed for me and my family while on the telephone. I was delighted.

I spent the night at the hospital. My mother took my son home with her. My brother and I stayed. During that time, my brother and I didn't have a strong brother-and-sister relationship. He felt that it was petty for us to not be speaking to one another.

He said, "Tracey, we have got to stop feuding."

He began to apologize for all the wrong that he had done, and so did I. We cried and didn't leave my sister's bedside. Her husband was there and he also cried.

My sister and I had tons of conversations. She said to me that she hadn't seen her husband cry. She said it with confidence in her voice.

I leaned over to her and whispered in her ear, "Jean, he is crying now."

During the night, she began to move her fingers. I thought it was a sign that she was responding.

The doctor said, "She is having a seizure."

Basically, they lost all hope. All I could think about was if my sister was born again?

"Lord don't let my sister die and go to hell. Please save her," I pleaded.

During that time, I couldn't eat or sleep. I went to church on the following Sunday. When my pastor called for a prayer line, I got in it. I told him that I was the person he prayed for over the telephone on Friday and my sister was still in the coma, needing prayer. He asked the whole congregation to point their hands toward me and pray. I began to weep. He told me to have faith. He said that he wasn't going to pray until he sees faith in me. I didn't understand what he meant. The service was so anointed. The choir sang and the musicians played. Suddenly, the spirit of God was heavy on me. I began to speak in tongues. The bishop laid his hands on my head and spoke in the name of Jesus. An indescribable feeling came over me.

I heard, "Wednesday." I questioned, "What is going to happen on Wednesday?"

In my heart, I felt that it would be the day she was to come out of the coma.

I began to scream and shout, "Thank You God."

I heard the congregation praise God with me. I felt so light and confident. Once I left church that day, I was finally able to eat.

I stopped over my mom's house to see her and my son. We then went to the hospital. I informed them that Wednesday would be the day. We were so happy. Because the Lord informed me, we had to have faith. On Monday and Tuesday I was excited. I talked to my sister and let her know how much I missed her and couldn't wait for her to come home. Wednesday morning finally arrived.

"Okay Jean, we are ready for you to wake up."

I kissed her head while holding her hand. Then, the hospital staff asked us to gather in another room. They notified us that she wasn't breathing or doing anything on her own. We had to make a decision. "How could this be?" I thought. "Okay, once they unhook all the tubes, she will breathe and respond on her own." I was sure of it!

The hospital staff removed the tubes. I was still excited, because the miracle was about to happen. Well, things didn't go according to what I believed. On Wednesday, July 5, 1989, my sister passed away. She died! I was devastated. How could God do this to me? I was so confused.

I fussed and began to tell him, "I give you my tithes and offering. I pray. I don't fornicate. I give you my time. I can't believe you did this to me."

I started to cry so hard that my bones hurt. I came home from the hospital and laid on my sister's car and cried and cried. My neighbor held me and then carried me into my house. I asked the devil and the Lord, I didn't care which one, to please kill me. I didn't want to live anymore. I intensely loved my sister. When I was little girl living in Barry Farms, she walked me to school. We held swinging hands, laughed, and took big steps so that we wouldn't touch the lines on the concrete. During Christmas, we used to have a Christmas tree contest. Her husband was the judge. Of course, she won every year!

I was devastated, so much so, that I stopped going to church. I thought that since I was a born-again believer, I wouldn't experience pain of any kind. What was the use of giving my life to God, only to suffer more? Well, I needed something or someone to help me deal with my pain. I called local information to get the city worker's telephone number. I called the house and his mother answered. She informed me he had gotten married that day and not to call there anymore. I couldn't believe it! I was speechless. If it wasn't for the pain of losing my sister, I would have been crushed. I didn't know he was dating someone.

Jean's service was beautiful. She would have been proud. I finally went back to work and they all made me feel welcomed. They were very supportive. I really appreciated what my manager and co-workers did for me. They collected money and gave me beautiful flowers and nice cards. I thanked them all.

CHAPTER THREE

LIFE AFTER ADVERSITY

My life took another drastic turn. I didn't realize there would be more dark days. I thought that after salvation my life would be trouble-free. It wasn't until six months after my sister's death that I truly understood why my sister had to die. She had two children, a daughter and a son. My niece was four months pregnant with her first child, which would've made my sister a grandmother for the first time. On the night of January 30, 1990, her son was murdered on the streets of Washington, D.C. The murder took place on a street behind my mother's house, which was down the street from where Jean and I lived. My brother-in-law knocked on my door before going to the hospital.

He said, "Tracey, this time it is pretty bad."

My nephew had been shot before and survived. I called the hospital several times to get an update on his condition. The next call was my last. He was dead! At that moment, I believed in my heart my sister had to die first. It's no way that she could have handled the death of her only son. Still grieving the loss of my sister, I went to another funeral.

We all adored him. We gave him a nickname when he was young and fat. He was known as Juggie. He grew up so fast, and the street life robbed him and us of a full life with him. We buried him just before his nineteenth birthday. Just like a lot of unsolved murders in the city, the murderer wasn't identified.

Once I came to my senses, I repented for my unbelief in God and went back to church. My mother talked to me and showed me just how good God was during our tragedies. I did myself a big favor by reading my Bible again and tried to enjoy life.

On April 11, 1992, the Saturday before Easter, my son and I went shopping, he played video games, and we stopped at a restaurant for lunch. We were having a good day. Shortly after we arrived home, someone knocked on my door. I opened it and saw that it was a family friend. We attended middle school together. She was a mortician. I was happy to see her. Before I could invite her in, she told me that my brother-in-law died. I screamed at the top of my lungs, and became very lightheaded. He was my sister Jean's husband. His name was Leroy Johnson, better known as Bunky. I called him Willie. He was jogging in Haines Point Park and had a heart attack. I was shocked! He was health conscious. He was in his fifties, and the family friend informed me that he didn't have an ounce of fat on his body. I called my family to inform them of the tragedy. I felt deep in my heart it was due to the loss of his family—his wife and son. His heart couldn't handle the stress caused by his grief.

After the funeral, I began to live again. In spite of the adversity we endured, I could still say that I loved the Lord and he was my helper. Several years past, and Sunday morning worship service was highly anointed. My pastor could preach the word. One Sunday he said that the Lord was impressing upon his heart to pray for generational curses to be broken over our lives. I immediately stood and got in the line for prayer.

He looked at me and said, "Daughter, God is going to use you. You are going to come into some money and your family will turn against you. The Lord is asking you to trust him. Trust God."

He made me look into his eyes. I looked at him and knew that it was the work of the Lord. I waited and wondered when it was going to take place. Where is the money going to come from? I prepared my mind to be ready for the next trial. I cleaned my life and parts of my mind. I began to spiritually and financially grow while waiting for the prophecy to come to pass.

My seven year old son and I took a cruise to the Bahamas. We visited Nassau and Freeport. We took lots of pictures, laughed, ate, and enjoyed our time together. One night, in the wee hours of the morning, at about two o'clock, I awoke to find that my son hadn't returned to our cabin. I got up and dressed. I walked all around the ship until I stumbled upon a nightclub. Who did I find sitting at a table with three other friends, laughing and eating cheese and crackers? He saw the look in my eyes. My baby was so excited. He immediately began telling me about the new friends he met and that the music was sounding so good he lost track of the time.

I said with clinched teeth, "If you don't get your rump to that room."

As we walked back to the room without talking, I silently laughed and thought, "The music did sound good." I chuckled when I saw how fascinated he was by all the lights and the glamour of the sin going on in the club. The trip was memorable for the both of us. We still speak of it to this day. My son and I have traveled to many places. We took drives to the beach and stayed at hotels for the fun of it or just to get away. We really had a good life.

I was an usher at my church. I ushered on Sundays, Tuesdays, and during special services. One day, as we were talking—having a mother and son chat—he told me he hated church. I was stunned! I thought back on how I used to drag him to the 6:30 morning prayer services and usher meetings. He wanted to play with games and toys, but I had him sitting in meetings with grownups. I didn't know what to say or do. Again, I prayed. Back in those early days of my salvation, I prayed when I needed or wanted something from God.

I asked, "How do I change this? How can I get him to like church? How can I make him understand?"

God allowed me to see in such a kind and gentle way that I couldn't do anything, only He could change my son's heart. How embarrassing. I always had the answers, at least I thought I did. Pride was another one of my many sins. I became humbled. A friend told me that my son needed to be baptized. So, I decided to take him to church one Tuesday night. I saw how the devil was using my son that evening. He fought me hard not to go to church. The devil knew it was almost over for him. My son got baptized that night and I was hoping that he was a brand-new person. The ministers prayed for him.

On Saturday afternoon, several months after his baptism, my son had some friends over for a visit. I was in my tiny kitchen preparing a pizza for them, while they were in the living room watching television. Someone changed the channel to the music videos.

My son spoke up and said, "We go to church and we don't watch this kind of stuff."

He took the remote control and changed the channel. My heart grew ten times bigger I was so proud of him.

CHAPTER FOUR

MY ROCK

She was five feet tall and feisty. She had beautiful curly, thin hair. It curled up no matter what kind of style she combed it into. She wore wigs so that she didn't have to spend time fighting a losing battle. In my mother's bedroom sat a wig head on her dresser. My sister and I drew faces on the head to make it look like a person.

She married my dad early in her adult life. Although they separated, she still managed to raise all seven children. My mother tirelessly worked as a chef and still cooked for us after standing on her feet all day. My dad seemed to have been a nice and kind man, yet, he was an old *playa*. I learned that he went back and forth to visit my mother and the other women. They slept together, he left, my momma discovered she was pregnant, and then, my sister Pam was born, and later I came along. My father left her before I was born. I guess she sincerely loved him. I can say that I love him too. In spite of how he treated us or didn't treat us, he did the best he could under the circumstances.

My mother was my rock. She was the glue that kept everything together. We always had good, hot food, nice clothes, and a clean warm home. My whole family was well-known. While rummaging through old pictures, I came across some certificates that we received for having the best lawn. That's how nice Barry Farms area used to be. Times were getting hard, and my brothers began to get into trouble, so Mama got us out of there. In my young eyes, she seemed to move us clear across the world. I was only seven, so to me, it was far. We moved down Nicholas Avenue, later named Martin Luther King, Jr. Avenue, which was still in southeast.

When I walked into the new house, I thought I would never like it. It was huge, and I believed we were rich! It had three bedrooms, a basement, and an attic. While standing at the top of the stairs leading to the basement, I smelled the mildew. I was afraid to go down there. Momma made me go down anyway just to see it. I went and found that it was also huge "Wow! What a great house," I thought.

I made new friends and enjoyed coming home to play. We had the best Christmas. Mama made sure we got most of the things for which we asked. While having many conversations with my mom, she later informed me that if it wasn't for the

Salvation Army, we wouldn't have had much. Since then, I give to that organization. One of my sisters always wanted a car for Christmas, which she never received. However, we got most of everything else we wanted and or needed. I can truly say that we weren't deprived.

My mother joined a church in southwest Washington, D.C. I used to pick her up around 1:30 on Sunday afternoons. Keep in mind, I didn't know the Lord during that time. I sat in front of the church listening to Go-go music at full volume. I lacked regard for the church. Every time she came out, Mama gave me one of her famous looks.

I often responded, "What is your problem, Ma?"

Little did I know, she didn't have a problem. I did. I thank God for my praying mother. I did eventually give my life to Christ. My mother and I used to go to church together. Sometimes it was fun. Regularly, I called her to let her know that I was on my way to pick her up. As usual, she came out of the house decked from head to toe. Mama wore the nicest suits and matching hats. I believe that's from where I got my style.

I often said, "Go head, Sister Jefferson…looking all clean."

Every time, she laughed and replied, "Get out of here girl."

We both had good belly laughs. After she got into the car, we hugged and kissed each other, and then she kissed my son. He was always excited to see her. I believe I was jealous of their love for each other. My son adored his grandmother. To him, she could do no wrong.

When I told my mother that I was going to have a baby, she said to me, "Now I can retire."

She retired to be my babysitter. Mama raised him from birth to age ten. Also, we used to go to dinner all of the time and grocery shopping, which I truly hated. I hadn't seen anyone take so long trying to decide on which cheese to buy.

"Really momma, can you just pick a cheese?"

I was so impatient at times. In 1994, I took a vacation day and we drove to Ocean City, Maryland. We stayed on the beach all day and talked like we hadn't spoken to one another in years. We read our Bibles and played in the water. My son played the most in the water. We ate lunch at a nice restaurant and shared stories that made us laugh out loud. It felt so good to have my mother all to myself. I often told her that I wanted us to buy a house together, just the three of us. I felt we should be together. She adored my son and he adored her. She spoiled him rotten, as if he was her first grandchild. When he was a toddler, she allowed him to jump on her plastic-covered couch.

"Who in their right mind would allow this?" I asked her. "If you continue to allow him to do what he wants, I will find another babysitter."

For a moment, she took me seriously, but still allowed him to jump on her couch and told him not to tell me. I guess that was a grandma thang.

When I thought back, I recognize that my mother was the best part of me. I loved her more than I could ever imagine. Sometimes things weren't always good, and we often bumped heads. I believe we were very much alike. We were both stubborn. I was still somewhat moody, and thought I knew it all. Sometimes, Mama just sat and let me have my grown-up tantrums. We apologized and became bonded again until we got on each other nerves, and repeated the cycle.

Late in December of 1994, Mama got sick. She was in the hospital during the entire Christmas holiday. My family and I usually had Christmas dinner at Mama's house. We decided to not celebrate the holiday until she came home from the hospital.

One day, while I spent some quiet time alone with the Lord in prayer, I began to cry. An ache was so deep within my bones. I didn't understand what was happening. I began to ask God what was wrong.

"Why are my tears so painful?"

After I stopped crying, I heard a soft and subtle voice say that my mother wasn't going to be with me for the next Christmas. I cried even more.

"No, not again. This can't be happening," I said.

While speaking to one of my friends at church, I spoke about what I heard. She began to rebuke the words that came out of my mouth. I told her I knew it was from the Lord.

Mama came home in January of 1995. The Christmas traditional celebration commenced. Everyone was happy. We exchanged gifts, played music, and laughter filled the air. Our family was all over the house and filled with joy. I loved my mother and her home. Because of the gladness that day, I wondered if I was wrong. Did I correctly hear God? Shortly after, in the month of February, Mama was back in the hospital. The doctors discovered cancer, which cut her life short at the age of sixty-nine. My mother passed away in March of 1995.

I never imagined being without my mother. Who does? In my mind, parents are invincible, and they can handle everything and still stand strong. A few months later, in May of 1995, I was informed about my job being downsized. I would be without a job again. I felt as if the glue that kept me together had melted and I was again falling apart. I really needed my mother. I was offered a good severance package. The job I held for 15 years was over.

CHAPTER FIVE

FILLING THE VOID

The first couple of days after being unemployed seemed to be quite disturbing. I felt as if I was being irresponsible. I didn't have to call in and lie about why I was not in that day. After a week or so, I felt better. I got my ten-year-old son up for school, made him breakfast, and sent him off to school. I then put on my jogging gear, drove to Anacostia Park, and walked for hours. On occasion, I sat by the water and cried or read my Bible. Other times, I sat on my front porch and read until my peace was disturbed. I was living a life of leisure. After all those years, I was finally relaxed. Sometimes I took baths or long hot showers in the middle of the day. At eleven o'clock, I got in the bed to watch my favorite game show. Those who know me well know which program. I loved the host. He was a fine, well-groomed, older man.

Life was getting back on track. Even though I was suffering because of the loss of my mother, sister, nephew, and brother-in-law, I knew my family was in good hands. I believe in my heart that they were all with the Lord. My mother loved the Lord and the word of God. I got that from her.

While my mother loved the Lord, she still had her shortcomings. Who in this world doesn't?

Before she went home to be with the Lord, she cooked for me and my son.

She often called me and said, "I've just made your favorite dinner—beans and balls."

Meatballs and baked beans were so delicious! She also made lasagna and chili with cornbread on top. On occasion, she fried fish, which was served with fried potatoes, onions, and green peppers. One of my other favorites was her egg foo young with her special sauce. She cooked for us so much that I had many of her food storage containers at my house. She had to call me to bring her dishes back to her so that she could fill them up with more dinners. That was something I didn't get from my mother—cooking. My sister once told me my son made a comment to his cousin that my chicken made his brain hurt. Now that was bad! I thank God for my mother.

It had been a month since my mom passed away and I still found myself crying every day, and feeling helpless and lonely.

Sometimes it felt like life was getting better, but then, there were days when I couldn't get out of bed. The month of April was near, and I had to face my birthday without my mother for the first time. I was a spoiled thirty-something year old woman who cried because my mother wasn't there. It was terrible, but I made it through. The dreaded Mother's Day was more difficult than my birthday…extremely difficult. My friends called me to wish me a Happy Mother's Day, but it was not the same. I didn't feel like I reached the level of motherhood like my mother. I did appreciate all of the calls and cards I received, and I thanked everyone, but I had to deal with grief in my own way. While I was lonely, sad, and depressed, I was vulnerable to the schemes of the evil one. I was low as low could get. I couldn't see the devil right in front of me. At times, I did see him, but because of my emotional state, I saw what I wanted to see.

I met him in May of 1995. He was funny, handsome, and just the right type for me and my son. For hours, we sat out on the hard, concrete front porch and talked. We had so much in common, including a like for the same movies and foods. We even lived in the same neighborhood while growing up. I was six years older and wasn't concerned about his age at that point. My void was about to be filled!

Four months later, we were engaged and planning a wedding. I believed that God opened up the windows of heaven and poured me out a blessing I didn't have enough room to receive (Malachi 3:10). Since the death of my mother and the loss of my job, I felt I received double for all my trouble (Job 42:10).

On December 30, 1995 I was a beautiful bride. The wedding was simple, yet elegant. My gown was off-white with pearls and beads all over. The top was off the shoulders, and I wore long matching gloves. My gorgeous tiara seemed to sparkle for miles. My makeup was stunning. My sister Jean's two granddaughters were beautiful in their hunter green and black suede dresses. The oldest was my maid of honor, and her little sister was my flower girl. When she saw the people in the church, she cried and wouldn't walk down the aisle alone. She walked with me and my son. My sister gave me a penny just before the ceremony. She heard it was for good luck, but I didn't believe in luck. I took it only because it was from my sister. My future husband's nephew was the best man. His niece was also in the wedding. I was the happiest woman in the world. My son, Stephen, walked me down the aisle. He was so handsome in his black suit. He was also ecstatic that he finally would have a male figure in his life. I believe I was happier about it.

In the days prior to the wedding, I was beginning to have some reservations. Everyone said it was normal; they were just wedding jitters. On the day I was to wed, I didn't feel quite like myself. I was extremely nervous. I cut my finger and the bleeding was slow to stop. I thought satan was trying to deter me. I wondered if it was a warning from the Lord that I would suffer. The bleeding just wouldn't stop. My best friend, Joyce, packed my finger with petroleum jelly, and that didn't stop the bleeding. I then put my finger under running water, and that didn't work either. We wrapped it with some cotton and I continued to get ready for the limousine ride to the church. Nothing was going to stop me from getting to the altar. My pride was involved.

My husband-to-be was also quite nervous. He had a terrible case of sweats, especially on his nose.

I told him that my mother used to say, "If a person sweats on their nose, it means that they are mean."

He replied, "It's just sweat."

Prior to the wedding, we sat and had one of our long talks about what life should and would be like. I told him that I would love to see New York City. The day after the wedding, he surprised me and we went to New York. He had made arrangements for my neighbor to keep my son while we were away. I called my sister from my cell phone to let her know that I was finally on my way to the Big Apple. I was so happy! The Christmas tree at a historic landmark in midtown Manhattan was beautifully decorated. Mobs of people were everywhere, just like in the movies. We didn't have much money, so our first meal in New York was at a fast-food restaurant. I was in love, and as long as we were together, nothing else mattered.

The night we returned home from New York, we went to church for the New Year's Eve service. Every seat appeared taken. A famous prophet was the speaker. He always drew a crowd, and so, we stood for hours. A close friend noticed something that I also knew.

She asked me, "Is he mean?"

I was defensive when I responded, "No way, girl, he is so pleasant, kind, and good to me and Stephen."

She looked past my falsehood.

She said to him, "Don't you hurt my friend."

His attitude changed in response to her comment. The church service was loud and crowded. I didn't pay too much attention to see if he responded to her. I made excuses for him and ignored his behavior. Yes, it was hard for me to face the truth about my new husband.

One early morning in January 1996, he left for work. I was a housewife. As I was asleep in our full-sized bed in a darkened room, I heard the phone ringer. It was his ex-girlfriend. He has two daughters by two different women. The youngest child's mother called and wanted to speak with him. I informed her that he left for work and asked if there was an issue? She stated that their daughter had been crying for her father, and she needed him to take care of her for a while. I informed her that I would get the message to him once he arrived home. In my selfishness, I didn't want to take care of her and didn't want the responsibility of caring for someone else's child. I assumed it to be a plan from the mother, but I was being tested. Yes, I failed. My attitude was terrible.

We had just gotten married, and I felt we had no time to bond. Each day my husband went to work, I was stuck with his little girl. I didn't know how to take care of a girl. I became angered when my husband came home from work and allowed her to play in our bedroom.

"This is not a romper room. Play with her downstairs!" I shouted.

I had her with me all day, and I just wanted to watch television in peace. He only spent about thirty minutes with her and then sent her to bed. We argued about her all the time. One Saturday, he wanted to go and hang out with his cousin. He got up and got dressed. His intention was to leave her with me.

"Oh no," I told him. "You better take her with you."

He took her to his sister's house. She was being passed around. After a few weeks, I had grown to love and enjoy her being in my presence. I began to teach her about numbers and the alphabet. We began to laugh a lot, and she always wanted a hug in the morning.

She watched me hug my son and asked, "Can I have a hug?"

My heart melted. When she first came, she cussed a lot. I had to let her know that little girls don't use those words. She was receptive. I'm not sure where she picked up that kind of language, but it was something I didn't want to tolerate. I felt like it was my duty to teach her what little girls should say and how they should behave. I polished her nails and cornrowed her hair. We were bonding, and I fell in love with her. I was certainly being tested. Unexpectedly, her mother called and wanted her to come home. The drama was over, and I had my husband to myself.

When the blizzard of 1996 hit the metropolitan area, it hit hard—covered in eight feet of snow. Everything was shut down. I couldn't look for a job. My husband had a sport utility vehicle, and people in the neighborhood paid him to take them to the store. He even assisted at the local hospital. He picked up nurses and dialysis patients. I was so proud of him. While feeling insecure, I questioned him about cheating with the nurses he picked up. To assuage my insecurity, one night he wrote in the snow, "I love you," with a big heart drawn around the word love. From his cell phone, he called me to the window.

As I looked down from my window at the words, I felt safer and was happy.

CHAPTER SIX

AS LIFE CRUMBLED

The bills began to pile up. He overspent what he earned transporting the stranded. Instead of paying the bills and buying groceries, he ate out every day. My last unemployment check came, and I had to begin looking for work. My life as a housewife was over. My neighbor informed me about a job. I interviewed for it and received a call for an offer. I accepted the position.

I thought things would get better. I expected that there would be no more arguing over bills and money. Our marriage was okay for a minute. We went back to our normal routine of getting ready for school and work, speaking to the neighbors, and driving off to start our day. We were able to shop for each other and surprise one another with clothes, music cd's, videos, or whatever we wanted. I couldn't believe it. I was able to shop again. I felt that it was what married life should have been like…work, shop, look good, and serve God.

One day, while sitting on my front porch, I was frustrated. The good times were short lived. I found out that he quit his job. I wanted to scream. I hadn't met anyone who suddenly quit jobs without having another one! I was bewildered. Unbeknownst to me, it was his pattern.

I went upstairs to our bedroom and said, "We need some groceries. We need to go to the store."

I could tell that going to get groceries was not in his plans, but I was determined to have my way. As he was getting dressed in his denim shorts and a collared shirt, in which he looked good, I kept pressing the issue that we needed to go to the store. I told him that he wasn't being the man I thought he should be and he was acting like a kid without responsibilities. The arguing continued until I decided I'd had enough. I told him that I hated him, took my wedding rings off, and threw them on the bed.

With one leap, he was in my face. He grabbed me by my throat and shoved me from the bedroom to the bathroom. I hit my hip on the doorknob, and then he shoved me onto the commode. He shoved me so hard that my back hit the rim of the commode.

He said with clinched teeth, "You better not do that again. If you do, I will hurt you so bad."

He said that he would kill me before he would let me go. I was speechless, and I thought, "This fool is crazy!" I ended up with a bruise on my thigh, back, and neck. After that incident, I collected myself and got my car keys. Whenever I had a difficult time or day, the first place I ran to was the cemetery to my mother's gravesite. He stopped me and started to cry. He pleaded with me and said he would never do that again. He didn't know what came over him and apologized. He also said he loved me so much that the thought of losing me scared him. He told me he never hit a woman before. We talked it over, and I forgave him. I told him that I had to go to the cemetery and I left.

When I arrived, I stayed for hours and cried. I begged my mother to help me out of my situation. I told her how sorry I was for the pain I caused her—for not being a better daughter when I hand the chance. I cried out to God for help. I knew I was in trouble. I hadn't imagined the same gentle person who polished my toenails and permed my hair could hurt me so badly. In response to his threat, I didn't do or say that again.

It took a while before things got a little better. I often held a grudge. He knew that, so he bought me cards and cooked dinner. He was a good cook, and made sure my son was well fed. When I came home from work, I didn't have to do anything. He washed and hung up our clothes to dry. He even laid out my lounge clothes, shorts, and a tee shirt. He rubbed my feet and gave the best massages. I told him he should go into business, but I would be his only customer. If he made a living out of it, I would have to be in the room with him. He laughed and said that I would never have to worry about him cheating on me. I loved his hands. They were so rugged and manly, but deadly at the same time. With that type of treatment, I slowly let down my guard. I was feeling happy again. We seemed to be a normal family, and things were getting back on track.

On one Saturday, my sister came over and brought her friend's pet for us to watch while she went out of town. I thought it was a good idea because my husband and son wanted a dog. He verbally expressed it. I didn't think it was a good idea because it meant that we had another mouth to feed. I didn't mind doing that for a couple of days. Well, when he came home, he had a fit. He hollered at my sister and me.

He said that he didn't want the dog there and wasn't going to take care of it. We both were shocked. He was so upset that he wasn't listening. I couldn't calm him down. When my sister left, our arguing escalated to the point that he packed his clothes as if he were leaving. He seemed to want me to stop him. I did stop him. I told him he had no reason for acting the way he did. The dog wasn't permanently staying with us. We were only keeping it during the weekend. He felt like a complete fool and apologized for acting that way. By then, it wasn't easy to accept an apology from him. I didn't believe he was sincere.

A week later, one of my dear male friends died from a heart attack. I was crushed! Knowing that, my husband was comforting. He drove us to the tidal basin. I sat in his arms and we both cried while he rocked me. He brushed my hair with his hands and rubbed my back. He said all of the right things at the right time. One minute he was abusive and the next he was sweet, caring, and compassionate. That was his method of operation. On the day of the funeral, as I was getting dressed in our bedroom, he appeared to be upset while he was ironing. I didn't bother to question him because I didn't want to get into an argument before the funeral. The ironing board was positioned between the two windows. I used to love looking out of the window while I ironed.

He turned and looked at me and said, "You are not going to the funeral."

My body tightened, and chills went up my spine. "This can't be happening again," I thought.

I said to him, "Just try and stop me!"

And he did try. He grabbed me by the arm and flung me across the bedroom floor. I couldn't keep my balance because of the high heel shoes I was wearing. I fell up against the wall. I couldn't believe his behavior. I reminded him of what he said—that he would never hit me again.

With a demonic look in his eyes, he said, "You made me do this."

I gathered myself and informed him that our marriage was over. I demanded that he be gone from my house when I got back, and left for the funeral. He was my best friend before I got married and was an usher in our wedding. I wasn't going to let anyone stop me from attending his home going service.

He also told my husband, "You better not hurt Tracey."

By the time the funeral was almost over and we viewed him for the last time, my husband walked down the aisle. He had the nerve to come. I was sitting with my friends. I can't explain my feelings of disgust and embarrassment. I got up and walked into the hall of the church.

He came behind me, gently touched my arm and begged me in what appeared to be in a sincere voice, "Please forgive me."

He then got on his knees and pleaded with me to take him back. He cried and said that it would never happen again. I was vulnerable. We both were emotional for different reasons. I lost my friend, and he had lost me. Yes, I fell for it again.

Days after the funeral, home life became calm. He cooked dinner. We sat and talked for hours, just like in the beginning of our marriage. He and my son played video games. He also escorted the neighborhood children to the park. While they were away, I caught up on reading or rested. Sometimes I chatted over the phone with friends. He usually returned within a few hours.

On one occasion, I was on the telephone with Joyce. He was in the kitchen making chili. He picked up the receiver, as he usually did to eaves drop or to ask me where something was that he couldn't find. He heard us laughing and thought we were talking about him. To this day, I still don't know why he thought we were talking about him. He was insecure. Joyce wanted me to come over to her house instead of talking on the telephone. She lived only seven minutes away, but we rarely saw each other. We hung up the telephone, and I started to put my tennis shoes on.

My husband came upstairs and asked me, "Where do you think you are going"?

I responded in a calm voice, "Over to Joyce's."

He said, "No, you are not," and grabbed my car keys.

I snatched them back. The force with which I grabbed the keys caused the bottom of the keys to pierce the bottom of my left eye. I became so angry and suddenly responded by hitting him as hard as I could. Big mistake! He pushed me backward, and I fell onto the bed. I bounced from the bed to the floor. He came over with the intention to kick me. He positioned his leg to possibly deliver a mighty blow, but unexpectedly stopped. I'm not sure what happened. I was as hot as a firecracker.

I said, "Give me my car keys because I am going out. I'm not your dog or your child."

He was determined that I wasn't going anywhere. I collected myself and began to walk downstairs. He pursued me. When we reached the dining room, he made me sit down. He was standing in front of me with his fist clenched. I saw the anger in his eyes.

I said, "Go ahead…if it makes you feel better."

He didn't hit me. Instead, he threw out the pot of chili he made. He was furious with me, and I was not afraid. I reminded him that he didn't buy the food in the house and had no right to waste or throw away any of it.

With determination in my voice, I said, "Give me my keys. She's waiting for me."

Without a word, he gave me the keys, and I left.

When I arrived at Joyce's apartment, she asked, "What took you so long"?

I looked at her and broke into tears. I told her what happened, and she was shocked. She had no idea about the abuse I had been suffering. She always told me that she thought he loved me more than I loved him, which was true. But that didn't excuse his mistreatment. Days went by, and the skin around my eye turned black because of my key jab. I had to apply makeup to cover the bruise, of which I hadn't worn.

-CHAPTER SEVEN-
I THOUGHT I HAD ENOUGH

Different kinds of abuse occurred during the next several months. Early one morning as I was getting dressed for work, he walked in circles, looking for something. I didn't ask him anything, nor did I assist him in his search. He was so furious with me for not being concerned for him that he put me out of my own house. Yes, he physically pushed me outside. It was during the winter and all I had was my bag and car keys…no coat.

I dealt with a lot of verbal abuse, manipulation, and control I also suffered financially. Although he was a jack of all trades, he had difficulty holding a job for an extended period of time. He was fired or just quit without any regard for our financial stability.

He often said, "You would have to pay the bills even if I wasn't here."

That was his justification for not working. One morning I told him he should leave if he wasn't going to help. I couldn't fathom taking care of a grown man who was capable of working. What kind of message was I sending to my son?

"Are you trying to put me out?" he asked.

He had the nerve to say he wasn't going anywhere and that as long as our address was on his license, the police couldn't put him out. Unbeknownst to me at the time, in the District of Columbia, the law existed.

I was truly suffering in silence. I had gotten to the point when I was tired of holding in all of the turmoil. I was about to explode. I wanted to tell someone, but I didn't know who to tell. Finally, I decided to inform his family. His brother and I got along very well. He was hilarious. While at work, I called and confided in him. I told him about the abuse, from past to present. He was silent.

Then, in a concerned voice, he asked, "What do you want me to do?"

I uttered, "Please get him out of my house because I've had enough."

He informed me that he would call me back. When he called back, he had a plan. He and his sister would meet me at my house to speak to him about the abuse and help him pack to leave. Well, my husband must have been looking out of the window from our bedroom. When his family arrived, he didn't come downstairs to greet them. For the moment, the mood was calm. His sister called out to him, but he didn't respond. She then went upstairs to confront him. My son was in his room with the door closed. My husband came running downstairs to challenge me. My heart was rapidly beating.

Angrily, he demanded, "Why did you tell them?"

I told him that I could no longer tolerate his irrational behavior and wanted him to leave.

He was heated, and asked for my wedding rings. As I started to take them off, his brother got in front of me.

Because I had gained weight, it was hard to get them off and it took me a while to remove them. As I was looking down, trying to get the rings off, my husband swung his fist to hit me. Just in time, I looked up and ducked. He instead hit his brother in the face. The punch was so hard, that if I was struck, I would have been knocked unconscious. They wrestled with him from the kitchen to the living room, got him down on the couch, and then instructed me to get out of the house. I left and went to a neighbor's house to call the police. My son also came out of the house, and I called him to me. Within minutes, the police arrived. I know that it was the Lord! I walked back to my house to inform them about my reason for calling. They ordered that one of us had to leave. My husband said he wasn't leaving. Even though it was my house, the policeman responded that I had to leave. His brother insisted that my husband should leave. Immediately, my son and I went in the house to pack. As I walked in my bathroom to get my toiletries, I noticed that he had drawn a bubble bath for me and placed a card near the tub. That was the kind of things he did after he was mean and nasty. Sometimes he cooked a nice dinner or came to my job with flowers in hand. I hated it when he did it because I knew his motive. Ludicrously, he stole my money to buy the flowers and cards.

Finally, he packed and we all left. Before I could leave, my brother-in-law came back to my house. He was in tears and asked me not to give up on him. My husband told him a sad story about how everyone always left him. He shared that when he was younger he wanted his brother not to move out of the house, but his brother had to leave. Could that have been the beginning of his feelings of abandonment? I didn't fall for the sob story. I informed him I would think about it and we all left. My son and I stayed at my best friend's apartment while she was away on a business trip.

Once again, life worsened. That night, I called to check my voicemail messages. I received a call from another dear friend. She asked me to call her as soon as possible. Once I called her back, she informed me that a friend for over ten years had been hospitalized and was in a coma. Her situation was dire. When I got to work, I called the hospital and begged them to let me see her. It was hospital policy that only family members could visit a coma patient, but they allowed me to see her. I rushed to her side, talked to her, and let her know about all that happened during the past few days. I cried and cried. The nurse came in to inform me that I had to leave because family was there. The last time I saw her smiling was at our wedding. Later that afternoon, she passed away. I was already dealing with the loss of my mother, the breakup of my marriage, and the death of my best friend. I couldn't grasp all that was happening. Shame, loneliness, and guilt were some of the many emotions I experienced.

I moved back into my house. My son and I readjusted to our current life. It was similar to the way things were prior to my marriage. My finances had gotten better, and we laughed for the first time in months. Then "Mr. Lonely" crept into my life. Just when I thought I could make it, I began to feel alone. Because I had accepted bad advice from some Christian women, I went to see my husband. We talked, and he told me he had been seeing a therapist. "Oh, okay," I thought. "That sounds good." He continued to tell me about the sessions and asked if I would be willing to attend with him. I didn't think I needed therapy, but I agreed to go. We met, and he drove to the meeting.

The place was run by students, which didn't give me a sense of security. The facilitators were not present in the room with us. They watched from another room. At the end of the session, they informed me that I acted like his mother, not a wife. They noticed that I wiped the sweat from his nose, which I always did. After that comedy hour, I was ready to go home.

Over time, we talked and laughed just like old times. I allowed him to move back in. Just what I thought I needed. The same day he reentered our home, I could tell that it wasn't going to work. I hadn't been a wife for long, and so I did what I thought was the godly thing to do. It was a big mistake. He became more violent. He went to counseling a few more times, then stopped going. He felt that after going to counseling, he was cured. I knew he wasn't.

My husband said that a fresh start might be the answer to some of our problems. He suggested we move. Yeah! It sounded great. We searched and found a new townhouse. No one had lived there before. It was a fresh start...*our* house, not my house. The first couple of months were like a dream come true. We seemed to finally have a good marital relationship. All of the bad times were behind us.

Not long afterward, he began to lie and didn't pay the bills. I discovered it when I came home from work one day, hot and tired, to find that we were without electricity. He walked in while I sat in my rocking chair eating a cold piece of chicken.

He asked, "What's wrong?"

"Nothing, dear," I replied. We don't have any electricity tonight."

He checked the lights as if I was lying and said he would take care of it on the following Friday when he got paid. I don't remember the exact day the power was out, but any day without electricity was too long. He did get the electricity turned on, but then the gas company shut off the gas. I must admit, I was about to lose my mind. My utilities hadn't been cut off for nonpayment—never. Momma engrained in my head to always pay bills first.

We had guests for the weekend—my two great-nieces. He apologized and said he could fire up the grill. To tell the truth, it turned out quite well. We had hamburgers, hot dogs, spare ribs, and baked beans for dinner. The next morning, he cooked bacon and eggs on the grill. Yet, we all had to suffer the consequences of his irresponsibility.

He started to stay out all hours of the day and night. My Lord and savior kept telling me to take my eyes off the man and to focus on Him. I started doing just that. It seemed to work. However, I came home from the hairdresser one day, and when I walked in the door, there was a huge hole in the foyer wall.

"Okay, what happened?" I asked.

He immediately pointed his finger at my son and began to tell me that Stephen was mouthing off. Although I knew he was lying, I still listened to him. I waited for my son to come home to hear his side. Each time Stephen spoke, he interjected.

I said. "Be quiet. Let him speak."

Both were at fault. Afterwards, he began to resent my son, partly because we had a close and loving relationship. The abuse was now being directed toward my son. It was one thing to be corrected for doing something disrespectful, but I wasn't going to allow anyone to hit him in an abusive way. The house was no longer my dream. I began to hate coming home.

The Christmas holiday used to be a joyous occasion for me. Somehow he managed to make that season a living hell. One day, a friend wanted to go shopping for gifts. She agreed to pick me up. I told my son where I was going, but neglected to tell my husband. He left the house as he pleased without telling me where he was going or where he had been, and so, I began to do the same. We were out for a long time. I arrived home close to eleven o'clock on a weeknight. He didn't like it one bit. When I came in the room, he had a chilling look on his face—the look that said he wanted to kill me.

He said, "The next time you leave this house and don't tell me where you are going, I'll *bleep* you up."

I turned and countered, "How many times have you left this house without me knowing where you were going and how long you were going to stay?"

"I don't need to tell you nothing," he replied.

As I walked into the closet, I responded, "My point exactly!"

He ran into the closet and punched me in my chest.

I gasp for air, then he stood in my face and demanded me to "Take off my panties."

In his sick mind, he was convinced that I had been having sex. Yes. I did it. I pulled off my panties and threw them at him. He examined them and threatened to kill me and whatever dude if he ever found out I was having an affair. The previous year, just before Christmas, he pushed me and grabbed my hair because I turned on the light while he was in bed.

I continued to live in fear which had detrimental effects on my life. While I suffered in silence, I didn't trust him anymore. He often wanted me to be open and talk. I knew that if I did, and he didn't agree with my claims, an argument would have ensued, along with the potential for a punch or being grabbed. I couldn't sleep—I had many sleepiness nights.

It wasn't unusual for him not to come home on Friday's until the wee hours in the morning. He then slept in the basement, and I kept a knife under my pillow and locked my bedroom door. I needed to be prepared for anything. I hated that my son was down the hall and was too young to help me and he shouldn't have had to. I felt fear, shame, and embarrassment, I often went into a closet or ran the water in the bathroom while I sobbed.

CHAPTER EIGHT

WHEN IS ENOUGH, ENOUGH?

Although we had some laughs, our marriage was basically over. He became more violent. He got angry over the slightest issue. He was paranoid and began to call me vulgar names. He even made me prove to him that I was menstruating. I discovered that he unwrapped my sanitary napkins once I left out of the bathroom.

He made sure to destroy everything I liked. I loved Sunday's for two reasons, church and football. I'm am a diehard home-team girl, and dressed every Sunday in burgundy and gold. Since I love football, he said that I was a lesbian. He found it hard to believe that I enjoyed and knew the game of football. I didn't assume that because he didn't like football he was effeminate.

I had planned to take a day off from work. Whenever I knew I was going to be absent, I normally gave a co-worker my parking pass. On the day before my absence, he drove my car. He was supposed to pick me up. My co-worker decided to wait with me until he arrived so that she could get the parking pass. We waited for over an hour. She decided to walk down the street to get her car, hoping that he would be there by the time she returned. Two hours passed, and I was furious. She offered to take me home. During the drive home, while embarrassed and humiliated, I began to tell her how much I hated being married and was unhappy. She was sympathetic and listened. I arrived home and was happy to be there.

My husband came home around midnight and said with a slight snicker, "Oh, I see you made it home."

With intent, he didn't pick me up from work.

I responded, "How are you?"

He just ignored me. While I was laying in the bed watching my favorite male gospel singer on the television, I continued to sing and clap along. He took a shower and prepared himself for bed. He had the nerve to ask me to turn the volume down on the television.

"When he finishes singing, I will."

I was surprised that he didn't react in an aggressive manner at that moment. He fell asleep. The next morning, he got up earlier than normal, turned on the television, increased the volume, and laughed out loud. I didn't say anything. I got up and went for a walk. When I got back, I noticed that he was angry because I didn't fall for his trick. I had known what the Lord wanted me to do, and that was to ignore satan's traps.

He said, "You think you are smart, don't you?"

"Yes," I replied.

I wasn't going to disagree. I am smart.

He leaped in my face and said, "I should punch you in the face right now."

I said, "Go ahead if that will make you feel better."
He didn't say anything. I trembled, because his blows were painful. The very next day, he made breakfast and brought it upstairs for us to eat together. I shouldn't have been surprised. It was his normal response after abusive behavior. By that time, we stopped doing nice things for each other.

We ate and watched a movie. After the movie, he tried to become intimate, but I wasn't interested. I got dressed in a pair of shorts and a tee shirt. I picked up my plate and proceeded downstairs.

He said with his head half-cocked, "You're not going to take my plate down?"

I looked back and replied, "I'm sorry, let me get it."

"Never mind, get the *bleep* out of my face. I'll take it down myself."

He was so mad. I didn't think he was angry because I forgot to get his plate. The real anger came because I rejected his advances. I no longer trusted him. I was afraid that he was having unprotected sex with others, and I would contract a disease.

I used to record televised soap operas. I hadn't seen them in a few days, so I went to the basement to watch them. Later, my husband came down with a video in his hand. He appeared to be on his way out to return it. When I looked again, he had positioned himself and threw his keys at me, I ducked. The drywall was punctured. He then ran in the hallway toward me; acting like a true demon!

He said, "Get up and fight me. If you don't get up, I am going to beat the crap out of you, so help me God." I said to him,

"God is not in this, so don't use his name."

"Get up and fight me," he repeated.

I got up, balled my fists, and began to silently pray, "Lord, you know I can't beat him, so what do I do?"

He punched me in my head so hard that my glasses went flying across the room and my head was turned halfway around. I grabbed his hand so that he couldn't hit me again.

He said, "Let me go."

I started calling on the name of Jesus.

All of a sudden, he dropped to his knees, cried and said, "Please help me. I don't want to hurt you."

He said he needed some help. I told him that I agreed, but couldn't help him. He exclaimed that all he wanted to do was protect his family.

I asked him, "Who is going to protect the family from you?"

For a brief moment, he was speechless. He started talking about the church, how I thought I was better than he, and how I thought I was perfect.

I told him, "I'm not perfect, and perfect in God's eyes just means being mature."

Well, he seemed not to want to hear what I had to say, yet our conversation lasted a few hours. He began to accuse me of talking over the phone to a man named James.

"I don't know a James. The only person's name I know with the letter J was Jesus and he may not be calling for me. He's calling for you."

He was angry and speechless at the same time. The television was still on, and a commercial was aired. The woman in the advertisement told her husband that she wanted out of their marriage. Still trying to provoke an argument, my husband turned and asked me if I felt like that lady on television. I was afraid to answer yes, but said it anyway. Before I could swallow, his hands were around my throat.

He said, "I will blow this house up with you and your son in it if I you think about having me put out or you leaving."

He got up and went outside. In the meantime, my son and his best friend came in because they wanted to go to the pool. I didn't know what my husband was going to do, so I asked my son to stay with me for a bit. I instructed him not to say or do anything just yet.

When my husband returned, he informed me that he was going to leave, but needed some time. He decided to temporarily stay in the basement of the house and stated that he wouldn't bother me anymore. For a while, he didn't hit me, but still did other intimidating things, such as creep upstairs, listen at my bedroom door, come in the bathroom while I was taking a shower, smell my panties, and pick up the receiver and listen to my calls. I also heard a clicking noise whenever the recording device on my telephone was activated.

For years, he accused me of cheating. I thank and praise God for keeping His word down on the inside of me. Despite the severe mistreatment I suffered, I kept my wedding vows sacred for the entire seven years. I hated him and how he treated me. I didn't want him to touch me. Do you think I was ready for another man to touch me too? We still lived together. For several months, I slept upstairs and he stayed in the basement.

Well, I finally had enough. I felt it was time to stop. One day, while I walking in my neighborhood, I recalled a question that I previously posed to a young lady years ago. When is enough, enough? I started to cry because I had no answer. I knew it was time to act. I sought the advice of an attorney. She informed me about the steps I needed to take, but she couldn't guarantee that the judge would grant me my petition. I felt trapped. That meant more abuse, hatred, and suffering. I informed another dear friend, and she offered to let me and my son move in with her. I knew that wasn't what I needed to do, but I had to do something to protect us.

While watching the news on television, I saw a women who was promoting her domestic violence agency. I called the phone number provided and informed her of what I was going through. She asked me several questions about my living arrangements, car, and finances. I told her about my house in the city and my current residence.

She actually said out of her mouth, "Can't you stick it out?"

She believed I had too much, and most of the ladies that came to their shelter didn't have anything. Also, she was concerned about my 16-year-old son. She stated that he could possibly get raped or molested by the women in the shelter.

I said to her, "No, I can't stick it out."

I reminded her about her advertisement, but she didn't have an answer that would help me in my situation. I hung up. I truly felt there was no way out.

I then called the county courthouse and asked about having someone removed. I was provided the necessary instructions. I pondered, wondered, and prayed. I asked the Lord to make a way and let me know if I was doing the right thing.

The scars and bruises were on the back of my legs, arms, and back. My blackened eye was the only visible sign of abuse. At one point, I contracted an eye infection called conjunctivitis. While at work, everyone kept looking at me. Some were genuinely concerned, others assumed my husband had caused it. The office gossip was that my husband did it. I didn't confront the women who started it because I would've thought the same. For the first time he didn't, and I couldn't blame him.

I kept having headaches because of the punch to my head. On September 11, 2001, I went to work late due to a doctor's appointment. I was fighting thoughts that I might have an aneurysm like my sister or the punch really did more damage than I thought. I thanked and praised God because the test was negative. The doctor informed me that I could just take a low dosage pain pill. While checking out of the front desk, the young lady asked me what I was getting ready to do. I informed her that I was on my way to work. She asked me where I worked. I told her in southwest D.C.

She said, "You can't get to D.C. It's shut down."

I looked at her as if she was crazy, asking, "What are you talking about?"

That's when the front desk staff advised me of the terrorist attack on the World Trade Center and the Pentagon. I was in shock. While watching her small television, which looked like something from a movie, I called my job and spoke to a coworker. I was in total disbelief. It took a while to contact my niece because phone service wasn't available. She told me not to come to D.C. My concern was for my family who lived in the city. I drove home and listened to the radio. I turned on the television once I was home. I got on my knees and started praying for people, those whom I knew and didn't know. I asked God to heal those impacted family's hearts. I called all my family members and close friends. I thanked God because everyone was safe. Later on, that day, I did my usual, which was to go for a walk. When I returned home, my husband was there.

"I was concerned about you today. I was wondering if you are okay since the Pentagon is so close to your job," he said.

I replied, "That's odd. I didn't get a call from you."

"Were you scared?" he asked.

"No, I was not scared."

He pulled me to sit on his lap and then asked, "What's wrong? Are you uncomfortable sitting on my lap?"

"Yes." I said. He looked at me with disgust and inquired, "So, when are you and your son going to move out?"

I jumped from his lap and responded, "When are you moving out?"

With a chuckle, he said "I'm not going anywhere."

I left the room in a huff, "We'll see about that," I mumbled.

The next day, I was afraid to take that step, but I was inspired after reading a book entitled *Do It Afraid*. I went to the courthouse and didn't look back. When he came home from work, I called the court house, and the sheriffs came to remove my husband. I watched from a neighbor's home. My son changed the locks. I knew for a fact it was really over.

CHAPTER NINE

SUFFERING IN SILENCE

I'm glad my story had a happy ending. So many don't get out! Please hear me. If the Lord speaks to your heart to leave someone who is abusive, do it! I looked at myself in the mirror. My complexion was an ash gray, as if I were dead. I had gained so much weight that I was over 170 plus pounds. At five feet one inches tall, my clothing size was eighteen. He drained the life out of me. I allowed it to happen. The reason I titled this book *Suffering in Silence* is because some of my story wasn't shared with my family and close friends. They only knew that I was unhappy. They didn't know to what extent. I endured a lot of hurt and pain. It truly took a long time to get over it. I still can't fully comprehend the reason for the abuse from the hands of the person I loved, admired, and once respected.

When children are involved, everyone suffers. My son battled with anger. He was also dealing with other issues that stemmed from the abuse. If you are an abuser, whether it's verbally, mentally, or physically, please know that you are damaging everyone around you. There are so many Scriptures in the Bible that speak against abuse: Here are just a few of them:

Colossians 3:19: Husbands love your wives and be not bitter against them.

Psalm 11:5: The Lord tests the righteous, but his soul hates the wicked and the ones who loves violence.

2 Timothy 3:1-8: But understand this, that in the last days there will come times of difficulty. For people will be lovers of self, lovers of money, proud, arrogant, abusive, disobedient to their parents, ungrateful, unholy, heartless, unappeasable, slanderous, without self-control, brutal, not loving good, treacherous, reckless, swollen with conceit, lovers of pleasure rather than lovers of God, having the appearance of godliness, but denying its power. Avoid such people. For among them are those who creep into households and capture weak women, burdened with sins and led astray by various passions, always learning and never able to arrive at a knowledge of the truth. Just as Jannes and Jambres opposed Moses, so these men also oppose the truth, men corrupted in mind and disqualified regarding the faith.

1 Peter 3:7: Likewise, husbands, live with your wives in an understanding way, showing honor to the woman as the weaker vessel, since they are heirs with you of the grace of life, so that our prayers may not be hindered.

1 John 4:18: There is no fear in love, but, perfect love castes out fear.

1 Corinthians 13:4-7: Love is patient and kind; love does not envy or boast; it is not arrogant or rude. It does not insist on its own way; it is not irritable or resentful; it does not rejoice at wrongdoing, but rejoices with the truth. Love bears all things, believes all things, hopes all things, endures all things.

Galatians 5:19-21: Now the works of the flesh are evident: sexual immorality, impurity, sensuality, idolatry, sorcery, enmity, strife, jealousy, fits of anger, rivalries, dissensions, divisions, envy, drunkenness, orgies, and things like these. I warn you, as I warned you before, that those who do such things will not inherit the kingdom of God.

Colossians 3:21: Fathers, do not provoke your children, lest they become discouraged.

James 1:19-20: Know this, my beloved brothers: let every person be quick to hear, slow to speak, slow to anger; for the anger of man does not produce the righteousness of God.

Ephesians 4:29-32: Let no corrupting talk come out of your mouths, but only such as is good for building up, as fits the occasion, that it may give grace to those who hear. And do not grieve the Holy Spirit of God, by whom you were sealed for the day of redemption. Let all bitterness and wrath and anger and clamor and slander be put away from you, along with all malice. Be kind to one another, tenderhearted, forgiving one another, as God in Christ forgave you.

Proverbs 6:16-19: There are six things that the Lord hates, seven that are an abomination to him: haughty eyes, a lying tongue, and hands that shed innocent blood, a heart that devises wicked plans, feet that make haste to run to evil, a false witness who breathes out lies, and one who sows discord among brothers.

For some, even though the abuser is out of your life, the results from abuse may be still occurring. You may have several reactions that stemmed from the abuse. For example, you may find yourself in a mental prison; not because you want to be there, but because you may not have completely surrendered all of the pain from the past or sought help to deal with your issues in the form of professional counseling. To find comfort, you may have found yourself eating more than what your body requires, as I did. Additionally, you might dislike being around people, fearing that they will ask intrusive questions. As well, you could develop a physical or mental illness. Did you know that fear *is* an emotion, and can become a mental sickness when we operate our entire lives based upon it? I once heard a famous woman pastor, a minister of the Gospel, say that FEAR means false evidence appearing real. After studying its definitions and Scriptures about fear, we may better be able to see how we've been operating in it. I first discovered I was dealing with fear after I often locked my door and stayed in my bedroom for hours, sometimes all day long. I didn't want to go outside, even on beautiful days. I thought about the times when he tiptoed upstairs and listened at the bedroom door with the intent of catching me doing or saying something that he could use against me. But, the devil is a liar!

I didn't have to stay in that state, always being fearful, and neither do you. Please seek help from godly counseling service; not just from anyone because others may tell you things that don't line up with Scripture. Make sure that what they are saying is scripturally based. When going through tough times, petition your heavenly father for a Scripture to help you. He is always waiting there for us. Many of us run to other people for a quick fix when our father in heaven is right there, waiting for us to call on Him.

My mind and body deteriorated. I later was diagnosed, after all was said and done, with osteoarthritis and high cholesterol. My heartbeats were also abnormal. For eight days, I had to wear a heart monitor. One day, as I was taking my son and his friends to basketball practice. I looked at my fingers and they were turning blue. My heartbeat was slowing. I didn't panic. I knew I had to quickly do something to get my heartbeat back to normal. I continued to drive the kids and prayed for the blood of Jesus. By the time we got to the gym, my hands were normal. I didn't cry until I got home. They were tears of joy, not fear. Since then, I managed to maintain a normal cholesterol level. I had to completely change my eating habits and exercise on a regular basis. After I learned how to properly eat, I cut out about 90 percent of the fat I was eating and changed an unhealthy eating habit, of which I was accustomed to for thirty-nine years of my life.

I realize that some people will read this book and may say, "If my man was abusive, I would just leave him." Or most popular, "I will never date or marry someone who is abusive."

Trust me when I say, "You might not see the signs."

If the abuse is occurring while you are dating, then run as fast as you can. If you decide to stay in the relationship, know that it will continue after marriage. If you see the signs after you marry, then seek help. First and foremost, seek God. According to Matthew 6:33, "Seek ye first the kingdom of God and all his righteousness, and all these things will be added unto you. When you decide to seek godly counsel, be honest. If one party doesn't tell the truth, then counseling will be in vain. You can't get good quality help when you accept the lies. I found myself in that state. We sought counseling at my church. He made the problem sound as if it was only a money issue and we were doing just fine.

The minister laughed and said, "Since you are just still newlyweds, this will pass. It takes some time getting used to."

Once we got in the car, I looked at my husband and asked, "Why didn't you tell the truth?"

He had the nerve to respond, "Why didn't you?"

"I'm not the one with the abusive behavior," I countered.

I believed that it wasn't my responsibility. The truth had to come from the person who has the problem. The offender must hear themselves say what their problems are, be it related to mental, alcohol, drugs, or sexual issues, so that they can be defeated. Holding it in does no one any good. It sometimes hurts because you know the potential in your loved one. Not all people stay in their unhealthy state. Plenty of people have overcome the addictive behaviors and are living happy and healthy lives. It can truly be done only when the person wants to overcome the habits.

If you are an offender, say this: "We can do all things through Jesus Christ that strengthen us," according to Philippians 4:19. If you have to say this to yourself five hundred times a day to get through, do it, and put the devil to shame. Don't shame yourself and your family. Make the devil the biggest liar that we know he is, and get help. Work on getting yourself clean and whole, the way our God created you to be. Remember, God loves you more than the people who are praying for you and wants you to be complete, in a wholesome state. Even though you and your family may love the Lord, you still might be having some deep seated inner problems.

Romans 7:15-20 illustrates when someone repeatedly makes the same mistakes or poor choices, and not able to get it together: "For I do not understand my own actions. For I do not do what I want, but I do the very thing I hate. Now if I do what I do not want, I agree with the law, that it is good. So now it is no longer I who do it, but sin that dwells within me. For I know that nothing good dwells in me, that is, in my flesh. For I have the desire to do what is right, but not the ability to carry it out. For I do not do the good I want, but the evil I do not want is what I keep on doing. Now if I do what I do not want, it is no longer I who do it, but sin that dwells within me." Hopefully, there will be some understanding of what you are battling.

In order for us to overcome those things that we struggle with or sins in our lives that are detrimental to our walk with God, we must perform an honest self-evaluation. We all have our struggles and need to be delivered from them, yet when we allow shame for our past behaviors to overtake us, we cannot move forward to a healthier life.

I still battle with procrastination and entertaining gossip. Rest assured, we will always need God to help us daily. We have to call on Him at all times. One good thing about God is that He loved us even while in our mother's womb. He will always love you, although others around me may not. He wants to set you free. We are like an onion, we have lots of unhealthy layers, it's amazing that we can stand up straight. Highlight or underline each one of the words below that describes your issues:

Abandonment	Cursing	Dry spirit,
Abuse	Critical	Denial,
Accusation	Confusion	Disobedience
Alcohol	Control	Domestic
Abortion	Complaining	Partners
Authority	Cigarettes	Exaggerate
Adversity,	Camouflage	, Eaves drop,
Anger	Credit Cards	Evil,
Attitude	Conceit	Empty
Agitation	Cynicism	Emptiness
Arguing,	Depression	Easily offended
Argumentative	Disappointment	Fear
Anxiety	Despair	Fretting
Addiction	Discontent	Frustration
Blame,	Discomfort	Falsehood
Blaspheme	Disease	Fake
Backbiting	Deceit	Guilt
Begging	Dread	Gluttony
Bragging	Drugs,	Greed,
Boasting	Disloyalty	Giving up
Bitterness,	Destructive	Gambling
Broken Heart	Doubt	Grief
Corrupt	Disbelief	Gossip
Confrontation	Drama,	Grumbling

Hate	Lust	Pitiful
Harm	Lack	Paranoid
Hurt	Lazy	Playful
Holding back	Loneliness	Pornography
Horoscope	Liar	Procrastination
Homosexuality	Lack of	Prisoner
Hardhead	Listening	Pain
Harassment	Money	Quiet
Impatient	Mourning	Quit too soon
Insecure	Mishandling	Quarrel
Idolatry	Messy	Rank
Idiot	Needy	Resist
Insulting	Noisy,	Responsibility
Intimidating	No sense of	Rage
Irritating	humor	Racist
Irresponsible	Nervousness	Revenge
Interrupting	Oppression	Rape
Jealousy	Optimistic	Robbery
Joking too	Overconfident	Sneaky
much	On purpose	Slothful
Judgmental	Overweight	Sleep
Kindness for	Patience	Suffering
weakness	Pride	Sickness
Low esteem		Smoking

Scared	Worry
Strife	Witchcraft
Sex	Workaholic
Snoop	Weight
Suspicious	Wrong motives
Sloppy worker	Whiney
Sloppy	Vanity
Stealing	Vengeance
Trust	Violent
Temptation	Yelling
Thoughts	
Timid	
Talebearer	
Tit-for-tat	
Theft	
Talk too much	
Unstable	
Unforgiving	
Unmerciful	
Uncaring	
Unlovable	
Uncontrolled	
Warfare	
Weariness	

Once you have identified those issues that may be problematic in your life, consider taking time out of *life* to study the meaning and behavior of each word. Then, determine how you will work to rid yourself of the very things that may block the healthy progression of your life.

CHAPTER TEN

MY SON, MY HERO

He was a senior in high school when the smoke cleared. I had a somewhat normal life again. Prior to that, my son had almost lost respect for me. There was a difference in how he spoke to me and didn't have direct eye contact with me. One night around 7:30, he and my husband were arguing. I was in my bedroom on the telephone. The television was on and candles were lit. I was feeling settled. I didn't hear them arguing. Once I heard them, I ran downstairs and tried to get in the middle of them. They were cussing at each other. I immediately told my son to be quiet.

He ran upstairs and yelled, "I want to move out."

I was trying to calm him down while my husband was yelling back and forth in response to my son. In the midst of all the confusion, I called my husband Boo.

My son looked at me with such disgust and said, "How can you call him Boo when this nigga is beating you upside your head? I can't believe you are so st…"

He stopped. He wanted to call me stupid.

I said to him, "Please say it. It is in your heart, and I know how you feel."

He began to wail and fell into my arms. I held up well for my son.

"It is okay to say what you feel. Trust me, I do feel stupid. I often ask myself why am I putting up with his behavior."

I told him that I didn't want him to move out and how much I really needed him and his support.

"Life will not always be like this," I said.

I asked him to trust me as I trusted Christ. I honestly thought we would live happily ever after. I thought we would have an awesome testimony for the saints and the unsaved so that they would believe God could deliver. I must admit, deep down inside of me, I was trying to get the glory. I wanted to hear people praise me for withstanding all of that and still come out with a husband. That wasn't God's will for my life. He knows our every thought, even before we do. I couldn't fool God.

Well, days went by, then months. They didn't restore their relationship. I remembered when my son once adored his stepfather. They used to dress alike, watch the same cartoons, and even looked somewhat alike. No matter how much I tried to cover for my husband by making up excuses for him, I allowed the situation to stay the same. I was trying to be the goodie-two-shoe girl, while my son was also suffering. I do believe my husband was suffering in his own misery. He sometimes cried to me and said how much he loved us.

I repeatedly said to him, "You don't love us enough to stop the abuse."

He didn't know how to respond. It really wasn't a question. I just wanted him to see reality. If he really wanted to, he would've stopped.

Our first Christmas, with just my son and me, was a poor one. Neither one of us had a lot of money for presents. I brought him what I could and he likewise. I wondered how my son felt about me through all of our trials and tribulations. I finally got the chance to learn his inner most feelings. My son wrote me a beautiful letter for Christmas.

He wrote:

Dear Mom,

Well, I must admit that this year wasn't the best year for us, but we are still together. I'm glad that it's just you and me together. We have been through some things over the course of time. So now that it's you and me, I know that we'll have our best moment in life. Thanks for being there for me when I needed you to be there for me. I'm glad we both have become stronger or will grow stronger together after all of this. Remember that all things happen for a reason. I know that we will have the last laugh overall. Truly, out of all of this, I thought that we would never be the same again. That is partially true. We will be better than ever before. I know that we'll have problems, but let's not let them escalate to a point that we can't control them. I'm sorry for all that I put you through, if and when I did it. Now let's have peaceful times together instead of the hell we went through. So to the greatest Mom in the world, let's have a Merry Christmas and a marvelous New Year's together, you and I. I love you so much, Mom.

Loved Always, Your Son
Stephen Jefferson

I cried all day. I can't express how grateful and proud of him I was at that moment. He isn't a perfect son, but he was becoming so mature. I thanked and praised God for him. He could've become rebellious during that time. He could've gotten into all kinds of trouble. He hung in there, despite the adversity. I prayed, and everyone who was concerned about us prayed.

I received his handsome senior pictures. It was hard to believe that my son was growing up to become a fine young man. One afternoon, he was bored. It was pouring down raining, and he couldn't go outside.

I said to him in a calm voice, "What's wrong?"

"I'm bored and I want to go somewhere," he responded.

Where?

He didn't know. Since I didn't feed into his pouting, he went to the basement to watch television. About a half an hour later, I asked God to help me because my heart went out to him. I'm never bored because I love to read.

I went to him, leaned over, and kissed him.

I said, "Just think, a couple of months ago we were living in turmoil. I don't consider this boredom. I consider it to be peace."

He became angry.

A few days later, he came in from school and said, "Mom, you know what you said to me the other day? I really got what you said. Now I come home from school, sit, and look around. I remember how much tension was in the air and how I hated coming home. Now I love coming home."

At that moment, I knew the peace of God was back in our home.

He was battling the abuse in his mind. We had plans to visit a friend who had moved to Florida. The day before we were to leave, two of his friends were killed in a tragic accident. He didn't want to fly to Florida. I made arrangements for him to stay with his best friend's family. That particular morning, he was acting very antisocial. While I was making his breakfast, he said something that was rude.

I said to him, "Don't hurt yourself today. I understand you are hurting, but you better put all things in perspective."

I began to pray while I was leaving the house. I knew in my spirit that something was about to take place, but I didn't know what. While I was at work, I received a phone call from the school counselor. Stephen was suspended from school for two days because of fighting in the classroom. I asked to speak with him and I laid him out.

He asked, "You don't want to hear my side?"

"You don't have a side. I will deal with you when I get home," I replied.

Once I got home, I wasn't in the right frame of mind to deal with his situation. I began to pack my clothes for my trip to Florida. About three hours passed, and I went into his room to find out what occurred. He informed me he pushed a girl.

I immediately jumped up and said, "A girl!"

He then told me what happened.

I said to him, "You are no better than your stepfather."

His eyes got as big as owl eyes, and he said, "Don't compare me to him. I'm nothing like him."

I was very disappointed. I went to bed around 9:30 that evening. After midnight, I heard a knock on my bedroom door. He asked if he could come in. Before he sat on the bed, he began to cry. He cried so much that the front of my nightgown was soaked from his tears. He cried for about fifteen minutes before I asked him what was wrong.

He then began to say, "I didn't mean to push her. I hate myself for acting like him."

I began to witness to my son. I let him know that his behavior was learned. People don't just become abusive. They have watched someone else do it, so they believe that it's a way of life. Because of what he experienced, the pent up hostility needed to be released. He chose the wrong way to let it out. After I felt in my heart that my son was somewhat better, I went to Florida. He stayed and went to the funeral of his friends.

Because he had supportive friends, he began to laugh a whole lot more. Since that incident, he had gone on to accomplish some of his goals. He was proud of himself. He had a good job working with a Christian company. He even helped me to pay the bills. He kept my car filled with gas, partly because he drove it. He was remarkable for a seventeen-year-old.

If you are experiencing domestic violence in your home please take the time out for your children's sake to get them professional help. Do whatever is necessary to keep your children safe and secure. Let them know that abusive behavior isn't the only way to resolve an issue. Listen to your children when they have something to say. They are smarter than we give them credit for being. If they don't feel comfortable around your partner, ask questions like these: What happened to make you feel this way? When did your feelings start to change? Why didn't you say something about this before? Please put your children first. They are a gift from God! They bring much joy and happiness. Seek help for them. I had some of the men from church to speak with my son. I am proud of myself for doing so.

When God speaks something in your heart, go with it. Only God can see down the road. We don't know what is going to happen in the next second, so stay in tune with the spirit of God at all times. If your son or daughter is not serving the Lord, please don't give up on them. Keep praying for them. If they are serving the Lord, this is a good thing. It makes for a peaceful household. It does my heart good to know how my son loves

God and the church while we were dealing with domestic violence.

CHAPTER ELEVEN

WHAT ELSE COULD GO WRONG?

My husband had a habit of wanting everything in sight. He pressured me into going along with his plan. He begged me to allow him to get whatever he wanted by promising he would pay the bill. Every time, I ended up paying the bill. We were broke and penniless. One beautiful morning while I was in my bedroom, he called to inform me that someone was taking him to the Department of Motor Vehicles so that he could resolve an issue with his license. He also stated that it would cost more money than what he had. Being naïve, I didn't hesitate to give him the money. I knew he was looking for a job and would need his license to get around. He knew I had money because I just received my unemployment check. From that point on, I became his financial institution.

He kept telling me, "I'll pay you back as soon as I get my first paycheck," and "When I get paid this week..."

Well, he sort of paid me back. Instead of giving me the money, he purchased something and called it even.

I was comfortable while living in Washington, D.C. I paid all my bills and had money left over for recreation, especially shopping. I also loved to frequently eat out. After marriage, I couldn't afford to buy a children's meal at a fast food restaurant. I couldn't figure out how two people who were gainfully employed couldn't afford to buy the necessities of life. I get drained just thinking about all that has happened. Although there are few subjects or circumstances that I struggle with speaking about, it's hard to put into words the hardships we experienced and the resulting impact.

The bulk of the abuse occurred while we lived in Charles County, Maryland. I receive a telephone call from my son stating that the electricity had been turned off again. While he was watching his favorite cartoon, a blank screen appeared. The remote control didn't work, and neither did the light switch. Someone knocked on the door. When he opened it, a man handed him a card stating the amount to be paid. I then called the Southern Maryland Electric Company to decide to pay the bill. I sat at my desk in disbelief because, they informed me the check he wrote bounced, and I could only pay by money order or cashier's check. The utilities were the only bills my husband had to pay. I was responsible for the mortgage, car insurance, food, health insurance, and miscellaneous bills. When he arrived home, I asked him why he didn't pay the electric bill. He said he was going to pay it on the upcoming Friday. I informed him that the electricity was turned off and I had paid the bill. I told him to give me the money on Friday. Well, I'm still waiting for Friday's payday.

Another time, I came downstairs to make breakfast for my great nieces and he informed me the gas was turned off again. I just changed my clothes, drove to the grocery store, and bought a lot of microwavable food, cereal, and milk. They wanted bacon, eggs, and pancakes with potatoes. Frankly, so did I. We couldn't take a hot shower. When I returned, he was sitting at the kitchen table, speaking with the gas company, and making payment arrangements. I didn't have a clue how much the bill was. They informed him the gas will be turned on the following Monday. I had to take my great nieces home early. I couldn't bear to have them suffer along with us. My husband kept apologizing and said how sorry he was that he didn't pay the bill and he would make up for what he had done. He made promise after promise and didn't follow through on any of them.

"Okay, dear, it's all right," I repeatedly responded.

I began to believe that I could do better alone. Similar situations reoccurred. We tried to make our marriage work. We laughed and began to call each other during the day, just to say hello. He even made some attempts to come home on Friday nights. I didn't know where he was or what he did. After he received his paycheck, he was broke the next day. My son and I usually went to dinner on Fridays or some friends and I got together for a good time. Due to his spending behavior, it wasn't long before I ended up paying for everything in the household. He did absolutely nothing, but eat and sleep…no contribution whatsoever. Because he didn't renew the tags on his car, I had to take him to work in the morning. I must admit, I hated it every moment of my life, and his, too. From Monday through Thursday, he needed me to take him to and from work.

On Fridays, he often said, "You don't have to pick me up."

One day I said to him, "Since you seem to get around on Fridays, why the same person can't drive you around Monday through Friday?"

Again, I didn't receive a response.

Once, he had this big idea that we needed an expensive vacuum cleaner. I told him that we didn't need it. He got it anyway. He kept saying that since he no longer had a car note, he would be responsible for the bill. As with his other so-called responsibilities, he failed to make the payments. We purchased a time-share in Florida. We didn't use it, not once. I had to mail them thousands of dollars to get out of the contract.

I became sick of him. I couldn't bear to see him come home. I looked forward to coming home on Fridays because I knew he wouldn't be there. On one particular Friday, I picked up the mail and opened the telephone bill. The amount due was over $1,200.00. I thought my eyes had deceived me. I almost fell to the floor in disbelief. I knew that it was a huge mistake. I called the phone company. After getting the runaround, I spoke to someone who could help me. She asked if I had a computer in my house. She began to softly speak. She informed me that the fees were from a personal chat line that someone had been using. She asked me if my son was using the computer. I asked her for the days and times, and it was always late at night. It wasn't my son. It was nothing but by the grace of God that the young lady waived the fees as a one-time courtesy. I cried and thanked her for her compassion toward me. Once we ended the call, I got on my knees and thanked God for His favor. When my husband came home during the middle of the night, I took the bill down to him. He acted surprised. What he thought he was doing in the dark came to light on the phone bill. I politely unhooked my computer and took it to my spare bedroom so that I could see and hear when someone was using it

It was time for him to go. Once he left, on September 12, 2001, I learned more about what he hadn't paid. I came home from work and found a note placed on my door. Once again, the gas had been turned off. Although $108.77 wasn't a large amount, I still sat on the steps and cried. I felt I couldn't handle another thing. I worked overtime just so that I could catch up on my bills.

The following Saturday morning, I called the gas company and was informed that the total bill was over $1,200.00 dollars. I asked the customer service representative why that amount wasn't indicated on the bill. She informed me of the policy and that I couldn't set up a payment plan because my husband wrote an unfunded check—it bounced. I had to pay $1,300.00 to get the gas restored. A few hours after I made the arrangement for the gas to be reconnected, the electricity was no longer on. New homes were being constructed across the street from my house. My first thought was that the construction guys must have shut off the electricity. I had a feeling that it wasn't the case. I called the company and the representative told me they received a money order for the month of September, but the August check bounced. I had to pay $350.00 in order to have service restored. I had forty-five minutes to get from my house to the electric company. I assured her that I was on my way with the money and asked if she could send a technician to reconnect the power.

I wanted the power back on because I was in the middle of making us a great dinner. By the time I arrived home, the electricity was on. Thank you Jesus and the electric company!

I just knew something else was wrong when while I was taking a nap when I heard my son call out, "Ma!"

I ran downstairs, and to my surprise, that very same night, the water heater burst.

As I was going through the turmoil with the bills, I felt I needed to go on a spiritual fast. I only ate raw vegetables and drank water. Earlier that week, I told my son that the devil was mad at me for fasting. I believed that I was beginning to get close to a financial breakthrough. Even though I felt like cussing someone out or just being rude and nasty because of all the chaos that had taken place, I was determined not to allow my flesh to control me. It wasn't anyone's fault but my husband.

By the time I got downstairs, there was a lot of water on the floor. I didn't know how to turn off the water. I called my brother Gary, and he instructed me. The water level was just about over my feet. I sat on the stairs and looked at my son, and we just cracked up laughing. He didn't know what to do or say. We had a good belly laugh that night. I had to pay a family friend to repair the water heater. The insurance company replaced the carpet and the drywall. I wondered what else could go wrong. There hadn't been a time when so many bill collectors contacted me at once. I didn't make a payment on the twelve-thousand dollar loan that I was forced to sign. I received phone calls every day, sometimes two to three times a day. I was under tremendous pressure. At the time the money was borrowed, he got seven thousand dollars in cash. I wondered what he did with the money. I was paying for the mortgage on two houses, homeowners insurance, the loan, an unused timeshare, a car note, and car insurance. I still had to pay for gas, electric, water, food, a vacuum cleaner, computer, and senior dues for my son. For the first time in my adult life, I felt defeated. He won! He wanted to ruin me. I couldn't stand the pressure any longer. I heard an advertisement about bankruptcy on a Christian radio station. I met with the attorney and cried in her office. I cried in front of complete strangers. For the first time, I had no pride or shame.

Staying in tune with God can save a lot of heartaches and pain. Not only can you suffer in your mind, body, and spirit, but you also suffer financially. If your other half is not a good money manager, proceed with caution. You can become bankrupt in more ways than one. If you can manage the monthly bills on your own, do so. If not, set up a payment system with your spouse so that you will not be put in a financial stronghold later. Unfortunately, I had to file a Chapter 13 bankruptcy. I didn't want to give up my house, I just couldn't afford to cover the cost for everything. I had a hard time getting caught up because of the debt my husband left behind. I felt ashamed. I only told a few of my close friends about it. I'm not proud of it, but I am human. I previously spoke against bankruptcy to a coworker. I learned that I shouldn't have been quick to condemn something just because I didn't understand it. God has a plan for everyone's life. Who was I to judge or know the plans of our God? After filing the Chapter 13, I was able to consolidate my debt, get back on track, and pay off the balances. I was also able to clean up my credit report.

In the book of Proverbs, it speaks about not cosigning a note. When you know someone who is not good with their finances, don't feed their every whim. Be strong and say no. If not, you will suffer for it later, as I did.

In Job 1:8, God said to the devil, "Have you considered my servant Job?"

That was how I felt after I went through all that hell. There will still be times when fear will grip you. Fear is only an emotion. There is nothing wrong with feeling fearful. Confess what you are feeling and say, "Lord I am trusting you to correct or workout this situation." He will in His own time. Be patient. Reach for the goals that you set when you were in the situation. If you were like me, you might say, "Once this is over, I'm going to travel, start a support group, or write a book." Do it! Don't let the trial or the pain that you've experienced go to waste. God didn't allow what happen for nothing. My pain wasn't pointless. If anything, there was a lesson in every trial. Get yourself up and start over. One thing that is different: YOU! Lessons have been learned and growth has taken place.

CHAPTER TWELVE

GET OUT

A victim is one who is subjected to oppression, hardships, or mistreated. Based upon the National Coalition Against Domestic Violence (NCADV), 20 people per minute are physically abused by an intimate partner. One in three women and one in four men have been victims from some sort of abuse. From 2001-2012, 11,766 American women were murdered by their current or ex male partner. Just about every nine seconds a woman is assaulted or beaten. Abuse can be in the forms of emotional, financial, spiritual, mental, and physical manipulation…by withholding to controlling those things that are pertinent to the health, safety and well-being of another. It's mostly about control and power over another. Abusers have deep seated issues, and we cannot fix them or stop their behaviors. They have to seek help for themselves. Until they are fully healed, no one should be in an intimate relationship with them, including you. You are worth more than you know.

Sadly, victims of abuse often dismiss, play down, or flat-out deny the violence they are experiencing, ultimately suffering in silence. Some will not speak out what they are going through because they want to protect the abuser because of their social standing, believe that they actually cause the abuse, have low self-esteem, or don't believe they are worthy of better. There are a myriad of reasons, yet no one should live under abusive conditions. I wanted people to like him. I didn't care about what they thought of me. It was my fault that I didn't take the time to really get to know him. Six months was too short. I knew as I walked down the aisle that it wasn't going to work, but I wanted to *make* it work. I was determined.

I have been punched, kicked, smacked, cussed out, threats made on my life, and my body parts were left black and blue. My money and checks were stolen, leaving me at times unable to take care of my financial responsibilities. I was afraid to come home and afraid for my life once he got home. I was left at work, spied on, followed, had my telephone calls listened to and recorded. I was alienated from my family and friends. I was accused of a lot of things. I've heard over the years that when someone is always accusing you of something, that means they must be doing what they have no business doing. I nervously jumped whenever someone slammed a door shut. I only wish I knew the signs of abuse before it happened. Abusers start off subtle, but it grossly increases over time. A few signs of abuse are:

- Being isolated from family and friends
- Withholding of affection, compliments, and money
- Unwarranted blame
- Irrational jealousy
- Excessive criticism
- Petty-minded abuse, including face mushing, walking way, moving the chair just before you sit down, causing you to fall.
- Unpredictable and indecisive
- Dehumanizing behaviors such as angry reactions to minor issues, being deceptive, lack of respect, manipulation, and/or dominance.

While dating, I didn't consider the initial warnings. Some warning signs of an abuser include angry outbursts, demanding their way without compromise, rude, possessive, threatening words or gestures, and overly suspicious. At first, their behavior is great. They want you to get to a place where you won't easily leave them. Those who abuse are bullies. They all want power over their victims, which helps them to feel better about themselves. They are often insecure, unrealistically needy, jealous, have to be right, oversensitive, quick to take offense, and blame others for their behavior. There are some underlying mental health issues that they must address to become well.

What I learned through my experience was that there is an actual cycle that an abuser goes through. First, the abuser gets upset about something, then the attack occurs, an apology comes afterwards with tears, some appeared real, other times it was crocodile tears, and then the niceties occur. He cooked a nice dinner…always. We had fun…until the next flare up.

There were somethings that I needed to do while I was in an abusive relationship to protect myself and my son until I was able to get out. First, I had to be calm. Because I didn't know how he was going to respond in any situation, I had to be aware that anything I said or did could have been a trigger. What I had to do was to ask him what I could do for him. That was to keep him from becoming angry and violent, even though his reaction was not my responsibility. I was more interested in our well-being. I also had stop being so verbal with him, especially when I didn't agree. I put a stop to the back and forth arguing. If you are in an abusive relationship now, please go to the Resource section at the end of this book for a list of agencies that can immediately assist you.

Abused people stay in relationships due to one or more of these reasons:

- Lack of confidence
- Shame
- Control
- Dependence
- Threat of abandonment
- Nowhere else to go
- Child care issues
- In love with abuser

If you are having a hard time leaving due to fear, lack of financial resources, or are emotionally dependent on your abuser, there are a few options to look into so that you get the necessary help. Consider seeking help from domestic violence organizations and support groups, religious organizations, county social services, or through legal assistance from the police or law firms.

Moreover, children are negatively impacted when living in an abusive household. Those who are subjected to and witnessed domestic violence often face emotional, mental, and social harm. Unfortunately, some grow into abusers themselves. They will need outside assistance. Consider their doctor as a first line of defense. If your children are also being abused, especially physically, a healthcare professional can help you. They will notice any bruises, cuts, scrapes, and emotional issues. They are obligated by law to report their findings and give you information about domestic violence. While in their office, discuss the findings and let them know what is occurring in your home so that you can get the necessary help for your children.

While fixing my hair one day, as I looked in the mirror I heard a voice say, "When is enough, enough?" At that moment I had no answer. All I could do was cry. I lived in fear for six long years. My stomach and shoulders were always tied in knots. I didn't know what it was like to relax. Being abused, I had to try and stay one or two steps ahead. It was time to leave, but I didn't immediately know how to get out. I wish I could say I have all the answers on how to escape, but I don't. I have only a few suggestions, but you must know what may work for your situation. Your safety and the safety of your children is paramount. I highly recommend that you contact a domestic violence organizational hotline where you can get advice or what to do and where to go for help. The first thing you could do is while you are someplace safe, make a plan and let someone you trust know what you are doing. Confide in someone that hates his guts, only because you know they will not tell him. Leave your escape plan in a place that is inaccessible to your abuser, like your work desk or give it to the confidant. Also, little by little, start packing a few items of clothes. Every paycheck, hide away what you could afford. Write out your will. If you are married, you can leave him $1.00. I was informed by an attorney that if you leave him something, it cannot be contested.

Also, open a bank account and credit card in your name only so that you can build up your savings and have an immediate resource without the abuser's knowledge. Do not use your home address because you don't want him/her to know about the account. Make an extra set of car keys and hide them outside if you need to quickly leave. Collect your papers and necessary valuables in one place. Let a reliable neighbor know to call the police when they hear loud noises and believe that you are in danger. And most of all, remove any weapons out of your home, including guns and knives.

Once you have about 30-60 days' worth of items secretly packed away, put into action your escape plan. You may even have to resign from your job and relocate. Also, change your telephone number and request an order of protection against him. Because abusers sometimes ignore the order, create several options so that he cannot locate your whereabouts. You can also take a self-defense class or go to the gun range and learn how to shoot a weapon. These are some suggestions. We have got to do something to try and stop them. We must fight back and stop allowing the abuser to keep us living in fear!

Unfortunately, in the Christian community, too many men in leadership positions abuse their wives. At one point in time, you could find solace in the church. However, some pastors are preaching and teaching the Word, but once home, they are mean and abusive toward their wives and children. Ephesians 5:22 says, "Wives submit to your husbands as to the Lord." According to Webster's dictionary, the word submit means "accept or yield to a superior force or to the authority or will of another." In my opinion, this seems to be the most favored Scripture of those who are abusive toward their wives. The contradiction is astounding to say the least. The word submit has become a cuss word in our community because of the hypocrisy of some church leaders. The meaning has been taken out of context far too long. Most women don't mind pleasing their mates, however, if asked in a mean, nasty tone, of course push back will occur. Colossians 3:19 asserts, "Husbands, love your wives and do not be harsh with them."

What if the first lady exposed the dirty secrets? I wonder how many churches would be affected. Being a first lady is a hard job, just like being a mom is hard. I haven't been a first lady, but I have been in close proximity of a few. I can only imagine the pressures of always having to be ready to witness to others and having the right words to say, while struggling with their abusive home life. Some of them make the job look glamourous, but behind the scenes, they cry and hurt just like us. Yeah, they look good, and have smiles on their faces once they walk in the congregation, but, truth be told, they are suffering in silence too. We all must speak out so that we no longer suffer in our own silence. Prayerfully, it will soon be over, you will be free.

It was September 12, 2001, the day after the September 11th attack, when I drove to the Charles County Court House to start divorce proceedings. I informed the clerk that I hadn't been there before and had no idea about what to do. She was kindhearted, and gave me some papers to write down my reasons for being there. While my hands were shaking, I put pen to paper and started writing every detail about the abuse and what I needed. She then instructed me to go to a court room and wait for my name to be called before the judge. As I waited and waited, I noticed that cases were being heard for people who came in after me. I wondered if they had my case or if I was in the wrong court room. I left the court room to seek guidance, and the young lady assured me I was in the right room and asked me to be patient. By the time my name was called, the courtroom was almost empty. I stood before the judge and could no longer be strong. I cried, and the bailiff handed me some tissue. I proceeded to discuss why I was there, which was to have him removed from my home. The judge granted my request, which was temporary, and informed me that two officers would be coming to my home to remove him. My husband had seven days to dispute the allegations.

"Why only seven?" I asked. "I want him out permanently."

He responded that it was the process. Both of us would be served with papers to appear back in court, and we both will get to tell our version of events.

"It's a possibility that he could be allowed back into the home," stated the judge.

I didn't understand how it could be that he might come home. Once I arrived home, I went to my neighbor's house. We watched him come home, and then I called the police to inform them that he was there. They later came to remove him, which seemed to take too long. I wondered what was happening.

Several days later, the sheriff came to my home to serve me the papers, which I was expecting.

The officer stated, "I can only image what you went through. We almost had to arrest him on his job due to him showing off so badly while we were trying to serve him the papers."

I didn't ask him what he did because I lived it. I went back to court for the scheduled date. He didn't. Therefore, my protection request was granted! I filed for divorce and it was finalized on August 5, 2002.

CHAPTER THIRTEEN

EXHALE

This step might be a little difficult for you to do, but at least try it, especially if you are free from your abuser. It matters not if you are in prison, living in a shelter, or homeless. You need to do this: Thank God! Please give God the glory because you are free from your abuser. Exhale! Take plenty of deep breaths and let it out, by means of crying, laughing, or talking about it to someone who is willing to listen. Keep saying to yourself, "It's over. He or she is out of my life." Although you may have *some* good memories with your abuser, you must completely severe ties to live a healthy and safe life. Let them go! Good memories may cause us to stay longer than necessary.

I used to justify my staying by saying, "He's not that bad. He just brought my son or me this or that."

It's a trap. Let it go. It was a manipulative ploy.

Consider taking a long, hot bath or shower, using a pleasantly scented product. Take your mind off your pain and imagine where you want to be. I used to do that all the time while I was being abused. Whenever I walked outdoors or exercised indoors, I often spoke encouraging words, "Trouble don't last always. I will be free one day. God said that I am the head and not the tail. I can smell the victory coming soon."

Keep pressing your way through. Don't give up because your blessing is on the other side (Philippians 4). Below is a list of the things that you can do to calm your spirit:

- Get a journal and write down all your thoughts and dreams.
- Imagine you are in your new home, apartment or a room. It's all yours!
- Imagine you are back with your family.
- Rent movies and invite people over.
- Have plenty of parties or just have friends over and sit and listen to someone else talk for a change.
- Give others some advice, but remember, don't be overbearing. Only give advice if they ask you for it!
- Enjoy everyone and everything. Life is so short. Live it well.

It is now time to put on the fruits of the spirit! God wants to fill your life with good and to live a virtuous life. To be virtuous is to be potent, efficacious, morally excellent, righteous, or chaste. For homework, read the books of Galatians 5, James 1, and Ephesians 6. In these books of the Bible, you will find wisdom to help you to stay strong, teach you how to walk, and show you what to put on. We not only have to put on clothing, makeup, and shoes…we have to put on God! The difference in putting on God is that we should not take him off. We should keep Him on every day.

Take off unrighteousness…

James 1:22-25 declares, "But be ye DOERS of the word, and not hearers only deceiving your own selves. For if any be a hearer of the word, and not a doer, he is like unto a man beholding his natural face in a glass: For he behold himself and goeth his way, and straightway forgetteth what manner of man he was. But whoso looketh into the perfect law of liberty, and continueth therein, he being not a forgetful hearer, but a doer of the word, this man shall be blessed in hid deed."

Put on the fruit of the spirit...

Galatians 5:22 states, "But the fruit of the spirit is: love, joy, peace, longsuffering, gentleness, goodness, faith, meekness, temperance against such there is no law."

Colossians 3:12 instructs, "Therefore, as God's chosen people, holy and dearly loved to clothe yourselves with: compassion, kindness, humility, gentleness, and patience. Bear with each other and forgive whatever grievances you may have against one another. Forgive as the Lord forgave you."

Ephesians 6:13-17 charges, "Wherefore take unto you the whole armor of God: Loins girt with truth; breastplate of righteousness; feet of the gospel of peace; shield of faith; helmet of salvation; sword of the spirit, which is the word of God."

Fruits of the Spirit (practice putting on these fruits)

Agape - Love	Gracious	Omnipresence
Charity	Gentleness	Omnipotence
Comfort	God's Love	Patience
Conversation	God's	Peace
(Godly)	Provision	Perseverance
Counsel	Honesty	Power
Courage	Hope	Prayer
Diligence	Honor	Protection
Discipline	Humility	Purity
(God's and	Hospitality	Quiet Rest,
family)	Humor	Quiet Spirit
Duty	Happiness	Quiet Time
Encourage,	Integrity	Repentance
Encouragement	Intelligence	Rest
Eternity	Jesus	Regain
Everlasting	Joy	Restore
Life	Joyful Laughter	Rejuvenate
Energetic	Love	Righteousness
Faithfulness	Meekness,	Salvation
Fearing God	Mercy	Seeking God
Forgiveness	Modesty	Sincerity
Friendship	Niceness	Self-control
Generosity	Neatness	Smiling
Gratitude	Obedience,	Strength

Trust

Truth

Testimony

Understanding

Unity

Wisdom

Wealth

Worship

Zeal

God has given everyone a free will—a will to accept or deny his love and the anointing. Do you know how to unconditionally love someone? Do you know how to accept a person for who they are and not for what they can do for you? Could you accept others' faults and failures? Do you find yourself feeling happy when your friend or loved one fails? Do you just let them go on their way when you see them about to make a drastic mistake? If you answer yes to any of these questions, your love is conditional. We should not rejoice over anyone's demise, not even our enemy. Believe it or not, we are to pray for our enemies (Matthew 5:44). This is what God's word says. We are to rejoice when they rejoice and we are to mourn for those who are in mourning.

Salvation is a free gift; the best free gift anyone can ever ask for. It does not cost you anything. Acts 3:19 says, "Repent ye therefore, and be converted that your sins may be blotted out, when the times of refreshing shall come from the presence of the Lord." If you want to be saved from the yoke of bondage, ask the Lord to come into your heart right now. He is waiting. His arms are stretched out. He loves you no matter what you have done. When he died on the cross, he died for the sins of the world. You cannot commit any act of sin that God doesn't forgive. The problem could be that you may not be able to forgive yourself. Once you repent of that sin, he is faithful and just to forgive your sin and heal your land. God unconditionally loves you. People cannot love as God does, but they can emulate to the best of their ability. They cannot free you from your sin. The best thing about salvation is that you have an advocate in the father after you submit your life over to him. You might commit an act of sin, but he is waiting for you to repent. Turn from your wicked ways and God will be there, waiting for you to draw nigh unto you. Try his love today. Trust me when I tell you, he will never let you down.

Even though we have been abused, God didn't do this to us. **It's not your fault!** You didn't know or fully understand what was occurring, possibly until it was too late. It's hard to get out, especially when you fear for your life and that of your children. During it all, God makes a way for us to come out. God didn't allow the enemy to kill us. Some people aren't as fortunate to get out from under the hand of the abuser in time. Man has been given free will, even to abuse, yet God helps us to get out from under an abuser when we are ready.

There are a few steps to salvation, even if your heart is bitter toward God.

The first thing to do is to **confess** what you have done, why you accepted poor behavior from another, your feelings, emotions, or whatever misstep on your part. Own your mistake so that you can be free. Say it out loud so that you can hear yourself say to God and to the devil that you will no longer be bound by sin.

Second, **repent** for being disobedient and going outside of God's will. For some of us, we were warned prior to getting into a relationship with someone of ignoble character but ignored it. Someone may have told you not to cohabitate with this person informed you about their history. Others may have believed that they could change someone.

Perhaps you said, "Well, it won't happen to me."

Well, it did, and this may be the reason for your bitter heart. Are you embarrassed because you sincerely tried to help? As I earlier stated, everyone has a free will. The person you may have wished to change wasn't ready to change. They didn't feel a need to do so. Even though they knew what they were doing was wrong, they weren't ready to stop. Have you ever noticed how a drug addict or an alcoholic has to lose everything, hit rock bottom, before they can reach out and ask for help. The abuser is the same way.

Third, **receive** forgiveness from God. Stop condemning yourself. Read Isaiah 43:25-26. You may have sincerely done what you thought was right. It's okay. Now you can have a love that you have always wanted. This love is from a man you can't see. When you walk with him, you can truly see and feel him in your life. Miracles will start to take place. You will begin to look different. People will begin to take notice of your transformation. You will even begin to love yourself. Yes, you will! Say it out loud now:

"I love _____(your name)_____."

Say this to yourself every hour of the day until you are convinced. Hug yourself. This might sound corny, but some people have never done this. Once you try it, you will feel and look funny, but keep doing it, and you will begin to accept yourself as you are.

It's not hard to receive the Lord in your life. Seek out a church that operates from Scripture and the Holy Spirit, but most important, develop a close relationship with God so that you can hear directly from Him.

Last, **reconcile** severed relationships. You shouldn't be the same person you were during your trials. When you keep the faith, you will be stronger than ever. I didn't think I would have made it out of my situation when my life was being threatened. I didn't know what was going to happen to me or my family. There should be a lot of joy, gratitude, and happiness because you made it out. Spend time with family and friends. If need be, reconcile the relationships that were broken during your struggle. You don't owe them anything but an apology. Don't beat yourself up because of the way you acted. Just be led by the spirit of God, and He will lead you to the people who need you. Keep in mind, your loved ones only wanted the best for you. Some knew the person wasn't the best for you. But, you had to find out the hard way, as I did.

One Sunday morning while I was about to get dressed for church, I wondered why I was attending that particular church. I made a decision. That was to be my last Sunday. While I sat in my car, I looked upon a man. He resembled my ex-husband. I gathered my Bible and pocketbook and strutted into the building. As I greeted everyone who sat nearby, I looked over to my right. In the next aisle, there he was. It was my former spouse. He saw me and then started to cry. I informed the lady who was in front of me that my ex was there and asked if I should go to him and say something.

She said, "Yes girl, cuz you looking good. Go let him see what he's missing."

We laughed, and I got up and walked over to him. He began to apologize for everything he had done to me. I apologized for my role as well. There was a brief and final reconciliation. Because I was still cautious about him, I ended up leaving the service early, just in case he had any idea about following me home. I haven't seen him since.

CHAPTER FOURTEEN

LOVING ALL OF YOU

As stated in Philippians 4:7, "What freedom to know all the yokes of bondages has been unwrapped from around your neck. What a peace on your heart and mind." I escaped without a hint of hurt, harm, or even danger. Wow! It is over. The devil hit me with all that he had during that time of my immaturity. How do you begin to become the new you? You can start by being thankful for God in every area of your life, especially for allowing you to wake up. Sadly, too many women are severally maimed or murdered by their abuser, even when they did all the right things to get out of the situation.

There are millions of people who suffer in silence. Domestic abuse is on the rise, but I wonder if those numbers are accurate. What about the ones who suffer in silence?

Some of our family members and friends aren't getting the help they need. My heart aches when I think about my past. Part of the new me doesn't blame myself. I encourage myself daily. Growth starts with you. How do you want your life to be? Only you can decide. No one can help you with this. Do you know the blessing is right inside of you?

After you have suffered from abuse—whether it's verbal, physical, or mental—you need to regroup. You must *find* yourself the real you. I used to be lazy, hot-headed, and a know-it-all. I now clearly see all of my mistakes and character flaws. Now I just try to help my son and others who want to listen. We have got to stop making the same old mistakes that lead us to nowhere. We have got to start making sound and sensible decisions. We are the life-givers!

Agree to love yourself first…all of you. If someone doesn't love you, it's their problem, not yours. God made you and He loves you just the way you are. Once you accept *all* of yourself and become comfortable in your own precious skin then you can walk with your head held high and be in total peace. Once you know this, let no one take anything away from you. Have you ever stood naked in the mirror? To completely love yourself, you must accept all of you— fat stomach, flat butt, small boobs, blotchy skin, short hair, long hair, natural or straight hair. Remove all makeup and your weave if you wear one. Look at yourself and say, "Hello beautiful," until you really feel it. Do this every day. When I first did this exercise, I cried and couldn't look myself in the eye. Now, I'm comfortable doing it.

When you think of love, what does it mean to you? Write all the things that come to mind when you hear the word love. When I think of love, I smile. To me it means beauty. It feels clean. I see pretty colors like light blue, pink, and white. It means an organized room with one special thing that only you consider beautiful. Love also means kindness, patience, and gentleness. Read 1 Corinthians 13. This book of Scripture is beautiful. There was a time when I didn't know how to love. I used to love someone only when that person did something for me. Now, I love people for who and what they are. Some people come from dysfunctional families and have a hard time operating in a healthy manner. Love is forgiveness. When some people do things, keep in mind that they might be reacting to something that happened to them prior to meeting you, and they are just now dealing with it. Don't take it personal. Love is everlasting. Do you realize that God loves you? He loved us even while knitting us. Isn't this amazing! Nothing we do will ever make him stop loving us, however, this is not a license for us to go out and sin or do something to test God's love. I can shout off this revelation alone! He loves me!

Love also can mean freedom. Love will not hurt on purpose. The greatest wrong came when Jesus was hung on the cross. The cross of Christ tells the best love story of them all. It also represents how sinful we can become toward someone completely innocent. Love will make you do things like buy someone a card or treat them to an ice cream cone for no reason. Love makes you feel like a giant; like you can accomplish anything in the world. When your mind and heart are free, you feel different. Everything becomes crystal clear, even your thoughts. Love is exciting and peaceful.

Loving yourself is taking a bath by candlelight while listening to your favorite smooth jazz songs. I love gospel music, but I listen to variety of music. Sometimes I just want music without voices. Love is calm. Loving yourself is not responding to the phone ringer while you listen to your heart. Love is fresh, like the morning dew or fluffy towels just coming out of a hot dryer. Loving yourself is the feeling of putting brand new sheets on the bed for the first time. Loving yourself is spraying a beautiful scent on your pillows. Love is the reflection on the wall from a scented candle being placed in a stained glass goblet. The refection on the wall is so beautiful. Loving yourself is listening to a saxophone or piano being played ever so softly. Loving yourself is putting on a pretty nightgown or nice silk pajamas. Loving yourself is sitting in the middle of your bed, with your legs crossed while laughing out loud at your favorite television show. Loving yourself is cackling with your best friend on the telephone. Loving yourself is being childlike, silly, and giggling. Loving yourself is eating a pint of your favorite sorbet. Loving yourself is accepting the truth about yourself, realizing that you don't have to have it all together. Loving yourself is tears of joy being shed because you have embraced who you are.

Only after you have learned to truly love yourself, can you love another…in a healthy relationship. What does a healthy relationship look like? Most of us don't know. It looks like two *whole* and very different people coming together to share a life in a functional way, not dysfunctional, which we have been used to for the most part of our past relationships. It looks like working *with* each other, no one having power over another. It looks like doing what the other thinks is best for them, not what we think is best. It is effectively communicating in love. It is allowing the other to be themselves and making their own decisions. We all have our own opinions, but judgment about a decision shouldn't be the end all. It takes a lot of time, effort, and consistent learning to build a healthy relationship. To create a nourishing one, both partners could do the following:

- Be trustworthy, respectful, and communicate well.
- Be able to manage conflict without threats or causing harm.
- Invest in the relationship and protect it.
- Be responsible for oneself and each other.
- Share wants and needs without the fear of shame, guilt, or reprisal.
- Have unconditional love.
- Attend to each other's needs.
- Be able to say "no" when necessary.
- Not be abusive whatsoever…emotional, verbal or physical.

There is no fear in love!

You made it. I made it. I lived to tell it. I just finalized my last name. I am now using my maiden name. Old things have passed away. Behold all things have become new. Take off the old man and put on the new man. I am a new creature in Christ Jesus. Yes! I even feel new. I feel the victory. You've got to feel it. It's an awesome feeling. I laugh more than ever.

I love to hear people laugh. I appreciate the fact that I can see, hear, smell, and touch. I love all of the senses that God gave me. I even appreciate the trials that brought me to this point. I love all of my family and friends who knew and supported me. I appreciate life so much more now. I strive not to take things for granted. Because we don't know when our life will be taken from us, we must enjoy where we are at the moment. "Weeping may endure for the night, but joy comes in the morning". (Psalm 30:5)

I've done so much over the years. I know God has so much more in store. He does for you also. Always remember that Jesus loves you and so do I. Thank you for reading my story, *Suffering In Silence.*

RESOURCES

National

The National Domestic Violence Hotline: 1-800-799-7233 (SAFE) or www.ndvh.org

Americans Overseas Domestic Violence Crisis Center: 1-866-USWOMEN (879-6636)

Washington D.C. Metropolitan Area

Domestic Violence Intake Center: (202) 561-3000 | 1328 Southern Avenue SE #311, Washington, D.C. 20032

The Maryland Network Against Domestic Violence: (301) 429-3601 | 4601 Presidents Dr. Lanham MD 20706

Hopeworks of Howard County: (410) 997-0304 | 9770 Patuxent Woods Drive #300, Columbia, MD 21046

Family Crisis Center, Inc.: (301) 779-2100 | 3601 Taylor Street, Brentwood, MD 20722

My Sisters Place: (202) 529-5261|1436 U Street, NW Suite 303, Washington, D.C. 20009

Joint Base Andrews Family Advocacy Program: (240) 857-9680 | 1191 Menoher Drive Joint Base Andrews, MD 20762

Still I Rise: (30) 868-4903 | 9015 Woodyard Road, Clinton, MD 20735 | www.stillirisemd.org

Community Advocates for Family and Youth (CAFY): (301) 390-4092 | 9201 Basil Court, Suite 160, Largo, MD 20774 | www.cafyonline.org

District Alliance for Safe Housing, Inc. (DASH): (202) 462-3274 | Confidential Safe House | www.dashdc.org

The Family Place: (202)265-0149 | 3309 16th Street, NW Washington, DC 20010 | www.thefamilyplacedc.org

Maryland Crime Victims Resource Center: (301) 952-0063 877-842-8461 | 1001 Prince George's Blvd., Suite 750 Upper Marlboro, MD 20774-7427 | www.mdcrimevictims.org

Thriveworks Counseling Alexandria: (703) 828-9054 | 6076 Franconia Road, Suite D, Alexandria, VA 22310 or thriveworks.com

Sisters4Sisters: (301) 552-7470 | 900 Greenbelt Road #300, Lanham, MD 20706 | www.sisters4sisters.org

I'm Bruised, But Not Broken, Inc.: (240) 245-0057 | Post Office Box 1762 Bowie, MD 20717-1762 | www.imbruisedbutnotbroken.com

Building Bridges Foundation: (301) 937-2556 | www.buildingbridges4u.org

Cell Phone Application

SafeNight: it's an app where donors can pay for a hotel for persons in need. An alert goes out to a potential donor when someone requests a safe place to stay. The app is a non-profit project sponsored by Caravan Studios. Sign-up just in case you need emergency shelter.

For offenders

My Covenant Place: (301) 577-7307 | 1300 Mercantile Lane Upper Marlboro, MD 20774 | www.mycovenantplace.org

ABOUT THE AUTHOR

Tracey Jefferson is a divorced domestic violence survivor. During her separation and divorce period, God led her to begin writing her first book project, *Suffering In Silence*, to help other women who may have been or are currently in a violent relationship. Her heart opened and her passion was birthed into helping hurting ladies, young girls and men. She volunteered as a counselor at a pregnancy center. She is very vocal about the issue of domestic violence and speaks to others about every opportunity she gets.

Tracey Jefferson is the youngest of seven, an aunt, a great aunt, a best friend, and a woman after God's own heart. However, her favorite position on this earth is being a Mother. Her son, Stephen is the love of her life.

Ms. Jefferson is a graduated Cum-Laude from Central Texas College. She currently resides in Maryland.

Website

www.traceyjefferson.net

Email

For public speaking inquires, contact Ms. Jefferson at:

traceyjefferson30@yahoo.com